# LETTERS HOME

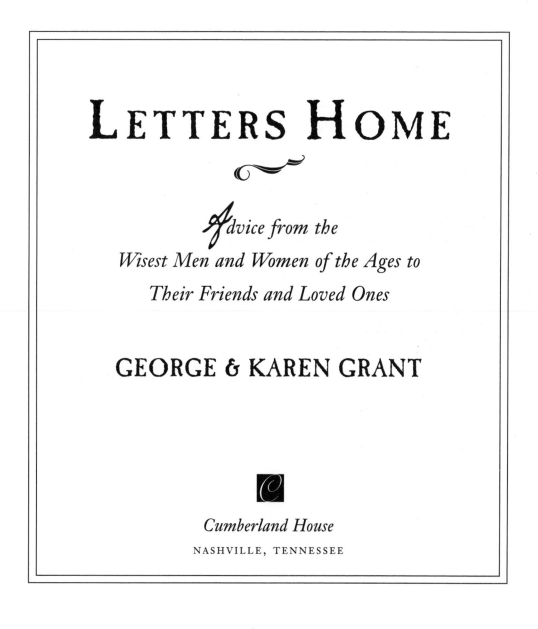

# LETTERS HOME

### Advice from the
### Wisest Men and Women of the Ages to
### Their Friends and Loved Ones

## GEORGE & KAREN GRANT

*Cumberland House*

NASHVILLE, TENNESSEE

Copyright © George Grant and Karen Grant

Published by Cumberland House Publishing, Inc., 431 Harding Industrial Park Drive, Nashville, Tennessee 37211.

Excerpts from Anne Scott-James, *Gardening Letters to My Daughter* (London: Michael Joseph, 1990) reprinted by permission.

Excerpts from Martin Luther King, Jr., *Letter From a Birmingham City Jail* (Atlanta: Juan Daves, 1963; copyright renewed 1991 by Coretta Scott King) reprinted by permission.

Excerpts from Corrie Ten Boom, *Prison Letters* (Old Tappan, NJ: Fleming Revell, 1997) reprinted by permission.

Jacket design by Tonya Presley
Text design by Bruce Gore, Gore Studios, Inc.

Distributed to the trade by Andrews & McMeel, 4520 Main Street, Kansas City, Missouri 64111.

**Library of Congress Cataloging-in-Publication Data**

Grant, George, 1954–
    Letters Home : advice from the wisest men and women of the ages to their friends and
  loved ones / George & Karen Grant.
        p.    cm.
    Includes bibliographical references.
    ISBN 1-888952-48-2 (pbk. : alk. paper)
    1. Conduct of life—Quotations, maxims, etc.    I. Grant, Karen B., 1955–    II. Title.
BJ1581.2.G675    1119
170'.44—dc21                                                      97-29581
                                                                           CIP


Printed in the United States of America
1 2 3 4 5 6 7 8 — 01 00 99 98 97

To Joel, Joanna, and Jesse

*"You are our letter written in our hearts,
known and read by all."*

2 CORINTHIANS 3:2

# CONTENTS

# ACKNOWLEDGMENTS

*"We cannot all be apostles, but we can all be living epistles."*
HILAIRE BELLOC TO HIS SON, PETER

Andrew Nelson Lytle, the great Southern man of letters once wrote, "Ultimately a man is not judged by what he has done or what he has written but who he has influenced—and who has influenced him." Our own testimony in life is shaped in large part by those who have exercised great influence over us through their care, concern, and counsel.

The fact is, we have been the recipients of good advice all our lives. Our parents, our siblings, our dear friends, and our mentors have all greatly enhanced our lives by passing on to us the vital lessons they had learned in life. To these we are ever grateful.

We have been particularly blessed by the wise counsel and friendship of Gene and Susan Hunt, David and Ann Drye, Tom and Jody Clark, Jim and Gwen Smith, Steve and Marijean Green, Scott and

Linda Roley, Mark and Barbara Thompson, Randy and Cindy Terry, Dale and Ann Smith, Stephen and Trish Mansfield, Steve and Wendy Wilkins, and Tom and Yo Clark. Their forbearance, graciousness, and kindness through the years has been our greatest encouragement. Though we suppose they are not technically apostles, they are most assuredly living epistles.

Ron and Julia Pitkin were enthusiastic about the concept for this book from the first time we mentioned it. We are grateful for both their constancy in friendship and their professionalism in publishing.

The soundtrack for this project was provided by Steve Green, Michael Card, Joemy Wilson, and Wes King while the midnight musings were provided by Scotty Smith, Colin Thubron, Hilaire Belloc, Edward Payson, and G. K. Chesterton.

To all these, we offer our sincerest thanks.

Of course, our deepest debt in life is owed to our three beloved children, Joel, Joanna, and Jesse. They have been our greatest source of and recourse to wisdom we have ever known. It should come as no surprise then that they were our chief inspiration for this collection of letters.

EASTERTIDE 1997
*King's Meadow Farm*

# INTRODUCTION

*"Write down the advice of him who loves you,*
*though you like it not at present."*
BEN JOHNSON TO HIS NEPHEW, WILLIAM AMES

Where can you go to get good counsel? Who can you trust?

Only rarely do most of us ever have the opportunity to get advice from the most renowned experts in any given field of discipline. We began to wonder what it might be like to gather some of history's best counsel during our son's senior year in high school. We wanted to pass on to him—and to his younger brother and sister—a legacy of genuine import.

In our search for sources for such counsel we discovered that the greatest men and women who ever lived bequeathed the fruit of their wisdom to their loved ones—often in the practical form of simple daily correspondence. Their extant letters are literally a treasure trove of wit, prudence, discretion, tact, probity, frankness, and sagacity. Writing, not for posterity, but for the immediate everyday concerns of family, friendship, and fellowship their comments contain a rich immediacy and applicability that some of their more carefully composed works actually fail to convey.

Living as we do in the fast-paced twentieth century where the painstaking process of crafting correspondence seems to have been all but superceded by voice mail, faxes, cell phones, pagers, and e-mail—we found the down-to-earth intimacy of these letters even more satisfying than we first presumed they might be.

We thus determined to collect a small sampling of the best of the best of this extraordinarily ordinary correspondence for our children.

Arranged by topic—such as love, money, character, work, temptation, faith, justice, and leadership—this anthology thus collects some of the wisest and wittiest letters down through the ages from some of history's most luminary figures—such as Charlemagne, Oliver Cromwell, Bonnie Prince Charlie, George Washington, Abigail Adams, Napoleon, Florence Nightingale, Charles Dickens, Mark Twain, Teddy Roosevelt, Albert Einstein, G.K. Chesterton, and C. S. Lewis. In the process, we not only were able catch a glimpse of the ordinary lives and concerns of extraordinary people, we were also able to discover the common sense solutions to the uncommon circumstances that each of us faces in life—regardless of our station or stature in the public eye.

Though we have obviously been very selective in our excerpts, in most cases we have left the punctuation and spelling as they originally appeared—unless doing so might somehow obscure the meaning of the texts or distract from their essential message. We felt that any remaining archaism, anachronism, or colloquialism would actually enhance their varied virtues.

Not all of the selections have stood the test of time—more than a few of them are from our own century for instance. But because this is a very personal collection, we make no pretense of selecting the very finest prose ever committed to correspondence. Instead, we have gathered together the bits of counsel that we found most apropos. We even included some samples of our own family letters. The idea was certainly not to put us on a par with the wisest men and women of history. God forbid. It was merely to establish our own perspective of the sundry sources from which wisdom may be found.

Though we began this project as a kind of "leaving the nest" bequest to our children, we felt the sage advice it contained might be of interest to others as well. So, we offer it as a self-confessedly subjective collection of our favorite words from our favorite folks—along with a few of our own words as well. We trust that you will find here hope and help for the day. But please remember, as the great American novelist Herman Melville once wrote to his daughter, "Good advice is one of those insults that ought to be forgiven."

# LETTERS HOME

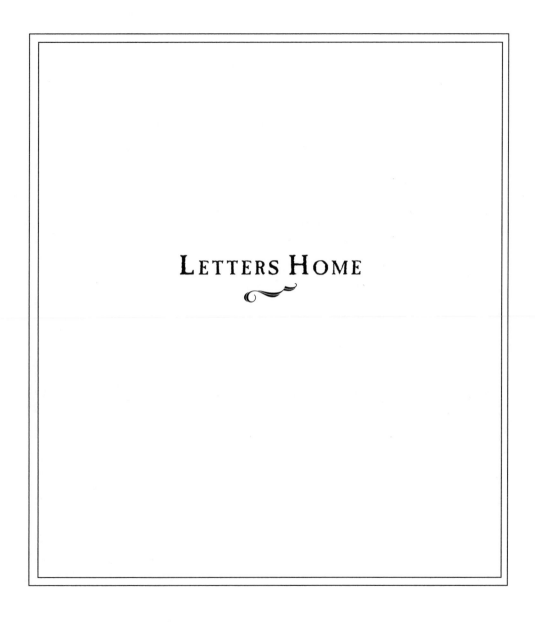

# Anger

*Many a man has been undone by his inability to control his temper. Many a cause has been lost because passion obscured vision. Self-control is among the greatest attributes that anyone can attain. It is not surprising then to discover that the wise constantly enjoin those around them to harness their anger. Here the great Scottish laird Walter Scott, the founding American statesman John Randolph, the Oxford prodigy Raymond Asquith, and several others weigh in with their voice of reason and words of wisdom on this subject.*

### SIR WALTER SCOTT TO HIS SON-IN-LAW, J.G. LOCKHART:
*Scottish poet and novelist, 1771–1832*

An angry man is seldom reasonable; a reasonable man is seldom angry.

---

### JOHN RANDOLPH TO HIS SON:
*American statesman, 1773–1833*

Reprove not, in their wrath, excited men; good counsel comes all out of season then: but when their fury is appeased and past, they will perceive their faults, and mend at last.

---

### PLUTARCH TO EURIPDIUS:
*Greco-Roman biographer and philosopher, A.D. 46–120*

Eat not thy heart; which forbids to afflict our souls, and waste then with vexatious cares.

# Raymond Asquith to his Oxford friend, Tommy Nelson:
*British scholar and soldier, 1875–1916*

Speak when you are angry and it will be the very finest speech you will ever regret. The greatest remedy for anger is delay. Indeed, a display of temper is the weak man's imitation of strength.

Here on the battle front, it is more than a little obvious that some men live and die at the apparent caprice of providence. Yet all the more die because they failed to hold in check the galling rage that war seems necessarily to induce. Woe betide the man who survives the trenches having failed to learn this lesson that ever enshrouds us here.

Anger is a despot that exercises an unrelenting tyranny over mind, will, and emotions. It is a kind of devil incarnate. Beware. Beware at all costs.

## SAMUEL JOHNSON TO JAMES BOSWELL:
*English writer and lexicographer, 1709–1784*

Life is but short; no time can be afforded but for the indulgence of real sorrow, or contests upon questions seriously momentous. Let us not throw away any of our days upon useless resentment, or contend who shall hold out longest in stubborn malignity. It is best not to be angry; and best, in the next place, to be quickly reconciled.

---

## SYDNEY SMITH TO A YOUNG CORRESPONDENT:
*English clergyman and humorist, 1771–1845*

We are told "Let not the sun go down on your wrath," but I would add, never act or write till it has done so. This rule has saved me from many an act of folly. It is wonderful what a different view we take of the same event four-and-twenty hours after it has happened.

# Character

*Character matters. It matters in all fields and endeavors. Generally, we moderns hold to a strangely disjunctive view of the relationship between life and work—thus enabling us to nonchalantly separate a person's private character from their public accomplishments. But this novel divorce of root from fruit, however genteel, is a ribald denial of one of the most basic truths in life: what you are begets what you do. Heroes don't simply emerge* ex nihilo; *heroes are forged upon the anvil of ethical faithfulness. Character matters. Here the great Russian man of letters Anton Chekov, the English champion of freedom Oliver Cromwell, the Southern statesman Robert E. Lee, and other luminaries emphaize this truth with passion and poignancy.*

## ANTON CHEKOV TO HIS BROTHER MIKHAIL:
*Russian writer, 1860–1904*

Do you know where you should be conscious of your worthlessness? Before God, if you please, before the human intellect, beauty, and nature, but not before people. Among people one must be conscious of one's human dignity. You are not a swindler, but an honest fellow! Then respect the honest fellow in yourself and remember that no honest man is ever insignificant.

---

## GEORGE WASHINGTON TO HIS NEPHEW:
*American patriot, planter, and president, 1732–1799*

Let your hand feel for the afflictions and distresses of everyone, and let your hand give in proportion to your purse; remembering always the estimation of the widow's mite, that it is not everyone that asketh that deserveth charity; all however are worthy of the inquiry, or the deserving may suffer. Thus is the mettle of true character.

# OLIVER CROMWELL TO HIS SON HENRY:
### *Lord Protector of England, 1599–1658*

I have received your letters, and have also seen some from you to others; and am sufficiently satisfied of your burden, and that if the Lord be not with you, to enable you to bear it, you are in a very sad condition.

I am glad to hear what I have heard of your carriage: study still to be innocent; and to answer every occasion, roll yourself upon God, which to do needs much grace. Cry to the Lord to give you a plain single heart. Take heed of being over-jealous, lest your apprehensions of others cause you to offend. Know that uprightness will preserve you; in this be confident against men.

I think the Anabaptists are to blame in not being pleased with you. That's their fault! It will not reach you, whilst you with singleness of heart make the glory of the Lord your aim. Take heed of professing religion without the power: that will teach you to love all who are after the similitude of Christ. Take care of making it a business to be too hard for the men who contest with you. Being over-concerned may train you into a snare. I have to do with those poor men; and am not without my exercise. I know they are weak;

because they are so peremptory in judging others. I quarrel not with them but in their seeking to supplant others; which is done by some, first by branding them with antichristianism, and then taking away their maintenance.

Be not troubled with the late Business: we understand the men. Do not fear the sending of any over to you but such as will be considering men, loving all godly interests, and men that will be friends to justice. Lastly, take heed of studying to lay for yourself the foundation of a great estate. It will be a snare to you: they will watch you; bad men will be confirmed in covetousness. The thing is an evil which God abhors. I pray you think of me in this.

If the Lord did not sustain me, I were undone: but I live, and I shall live, to the good pleasure of His grace; I find mercy at need. The God of all grace keep you. I rest, your loving father. My love to my dear Daughter (whom I frequently pray for) and to all friends.

## Patrick Henry to his pupil, Donald MacCarran:

*American patriot, statesman, and orator, 1736–1799*

Character is what you are when no one is watching.

---

## Robert E. Lee to his daughter Anne:

*American general and educator, 1807–1870*

I take advantage of your gracious permission to write to you, and there is no telling how far my feelings might carry me were I not limited by the conveyance furnished by the Mim's letter, which lies before me, and which must, the Mim says so, go in this morning's mail. But my limited time does not diminish my affection for you, Annie, nor prevent my thinking of you and wishing for you. I long to see you through the dilatory nights. At dawn when I rise, and all day, my thoughts revert to you in expressions that you cannot hear or I repeat.

I hope you will always appear to me as you are now painted on my heart, and that you will endeavor to improve and so conduct yourself as to make you happy and me joyful all our lives. Diligent and earnest attention to all your duties can only accomplish this. I am told you are growing very tall, and I hope very straight. I do not know what the Cadets will say if the Superintendent's children do not practice what he demands of them. They will naturally say he had better attend to his own before he corrects other people's children, and as he permits his to stoop it is hard he will not allow them. You and Agnes must not, therefore, bring me into discredit with my young friends, or give them reason to think that I require more of them than of my own.

I presume your mother has told all about us, our neighbors and our affairs. And indeed she may have done that and not said much either, so far as I know. But we are all well and have much to be grateful for. Tomorrow we anticipate the pleasure of your brother's company, which is always a source of pleasure to us. It is the only time we see him, except when the Corps come under my view at some of their exercises, when my eye is sure to distinguish him among his comrades and follow him over the plain. Give much love to your dear grandmother, grandfather, Agnes, Miss Sue, Lucretia, and all friends, including the servants. Write sometimes, and think always of your affectionate father.

# Queen Charlotte Sophia to her third son, William:
### ❦ *Wife of England's George III, 1744–1818* ❧

I am very happy to find by both your letters that you are perfectly well and so much amused, but cannot help saying how sorry I am to see that you continue still to harbour such unaccountable dislikes to those about you. Your reasons for liking and disliking are in general so trifling and frivolous that the best judgment one could form upon them would be that of youthful volatility, but when one knows you to be twenty years of age this very month, this excuse can no longer be made and severer judgments must arise, which can be no less than the want of a good heart, want of understanding, ambition, vanity, willfulness and an uncommon share of caprice, which imperceptibly will lead you to be what you will be ashamed to hear, a true trifling character, which is the most despicable of all things in the world, and the higher the rank the more it is observed; and it is surprising that with the proofs you give to the world of your offensive pride you do not feel the necessity of a proper behaviour. Want of decency is want of sense, and can there be a greater proof of that, than your shunning the company of those whose experience could alone direct and guide you, and the choice you make, in your acquaintance of every young man that comes to see Germany.

Believe me, there is not so great a fool and so bad a man but he sees your faults and carries you as he finds you wherever he goes, and that is your case already, for it is amazing how your indifference of behaviour is talked of both here and abroad, and the world so far is just in attributing it to your want of minding the advice of proper people, and the great opinion you have of yourself. Cease, I beseech you, to be a great-little man, which in reality is nothing at all, and return to those who are put about you in order to guide you.

Do not think that all Princes share alike. The situation of some is unfortunately such, that they can never be in a way to hear their real faults as it is people's interest to keep them ignorant of it, but a younger brother can never be in that dilemma, for though you are the King's third son, brought up in an honorable profession, I do assure you you will not have it in your power to make people believe that your pretensions to a thing makes you worthy of it if you are not, nay, what is more to be feared is that they will encourage you to think so in order to make your fall the sorer, and in the end profit by your ignorance.

Try for the future to be more reasonable. Make no promises but act a right, honorable, open part; think time is their company, and

leave vice and folly to those who think but of the present & not of
hereafter. Choose to be a useful member of society and make yourself more respected through your decency and good behaviour than
by your rank. This respect of rank is like that paid to the idols, but
that which is gained by a uniform continual upright conduct is everlasting.

Whatever I can contribute to your reform I am very ready to do
at all times, but I beseech you make no more promises, for they fill
your letters but take no effect upon yourself. Before you answer I
beg you will reflect a little and consider whether it is not more for
your good to have recourse to Budie's advice and to follow it than to
be directed by your own little nonsensical volatile head. *Adieu tout à
vous.*

ALEXANDER GRAHAM BELL TO HIS COUSIN:
*Scottish-born American inventor of the telephone, 1847–1922*

Thinking well is wise, planning well is wiser, but doing well is wisest of all.

---

H.G. WELLS TO GEORGE BERNARD SHAW:
*British writer, 1866–1947*

A bad conscience has a good memory.

# Children

*Our children are our greatest legacy. They are our most valu-
able investment. There is no better hope, no surer joy, and no
finer accomplishment than having set the next generation upon
the narrow road. The tyranny of the urgent may constantly
hark diverting attentions, but this is the most satisfying of all
occupations. Here the mother of two of the greatest men
England ever produced, John and Charles Wesley, offers
her wise perspective on child-rearing.*

# SUSANNA WESLEY TO HER SON JOHN:

*English mother of nineteen, including two great evangelists, 1669–1742*

According to your desire, I have collected the principal rules I observed in educating my family.

The children were always put into a regular method of living, in such things as they were capable of, from their birth; as in dressing and undressing, changing their linen, etc. The first quarter commonly passed in sleep. After that they were, if possible, laid into their cradles awake, and rocked to sleep, and so they were kept rocking till it was time for them to awake. This was done to bring them to a regular course of sleeping, which at first was three hours in the morning, and three in the afternoon; afterwards two hours till they needed none at all. When turned a year old (and some before) they were taught to fear the rod and to cry softly, by which means they escaped abundance of correction which they might otherwise have had, and that most odious noise of the crying of children was rarely heard in the house, but the family usually lived in as much quietness as if there had not been a child among them.

As soon as they were grown pretty strong they were confined to three meals a day. At dinner their little table and chairs were set by ours, where they could be overlooked; and they were suffered to eat and drink (small beer) as much as they would, but not to call for anything. If they wanted aught they used to whisper to the maid that attended them, who came and spake to me; and as soon as they could handle a knife and fork they were set to our table. They were never suffered to choose their meat, but always made to eat such things as were provided for the family. Mornings they always had spoon meat; sometimes at nights. But whatever they had, they were never permitted at those meals to eat of more than one thing, and of that sparingly enough. Drinking or eating between meals was never allowed, unless in case of sickness, which seldom happened. Nor were they suffered to go into the kitchen to ask anything of the servants when they were at meat: if it was known they did so, they were certainly beat, and the servants reprimanded.

At six as soon as family prayer was over, they had their supper; at seven the maid washed them, and, beginning at the youngest, she undressed and got them all to bed by eight, at which time she left them in their several rooms awake, for there was no such thing allowed of in our house as sitting by a child till it fell asleep.

They were so constantly used to eat and drink what was given them that when any of them was ill there was no difficulty in making them take the most unpleasant medicine; for they durst not refuse it, though some of them would presently throw it up. This I mention to show that a person may be taught to take anything, though it be never so much against his stomach.

In order to form the minds of children, the first thing to be done is to conquer their will and bring them to an obedient temper. To inform the understanding is a work of time, and must with children proceed by slow degrees, as they are able to bear it; but the subjecting the will is a thing which must be done at once, and the sooner the better, for by neglecting timely correction they will contract a stubbornness and obstinacy which are hardly ever after conquered, and never without using such severity as would be as painful to me as to the child. In the esteem of the world they pass for kind and indulgent whom I call cruel parents, who permit their children to get habits which they know must be afterwards broken. Nay, some are so stupidly fond as in sport to teach their children to do things which in a while after they have severely beaten them for doing. When a child is corrected it must be conquered, and this will be no hard matter to do, if it be not grown headstrong by too much indulgence. And when the will of a child is totally subdued, and it is brought to revere and stand in awe of the parents, then a great many childish follies and inadvertences may be passed by. Some should be overlooked and taken no notice of, and others mildly reproved; but no willful transgression ought ever to be forgiven children without chastisement less or more, as the nature and circumstances of the case may require. I insist on the conquering of the will of children betimes, because this is the only strong and rational foundation of a religious education, without which both precept and example will be ineffectual. But when this is thoroughly done, then a child is capable of being governed by the reason and piety of its parents, till its own understanding comes to maturity, and the principles of religion have taken root in the mind.

I cannot yet dismiss the subject. As self-will is the root of all sin and misery, so whatever cherishes this in children ensures their after wretchedness and irreligion: whatever checks and mortifies it, promotes their future happiness and piety. This is still more evident if we farther consider that religion is nothing else than doing the will of God and not our own; that the one grand impediment to our temporal and eternal happiness being this self-will, no indulgence of it can be trivial, no denial unprofitable. Heaven or hell depends on this alone, so that the parent who studies to subdue it in his child works together with God in the renewing and saving a soul. The parent who indulges it does the Devil's work; makes religion impracticable, salvation unattainable, and does all that in him lies to damn his child body and soul forever.

Our children were taught as soon as they could speak the Lord's prayer, which they were made to say at rising and bedtime constantly, to which, as they grew bigger, were added a short prayer for their parents, and some collects, a short catechism, and some portion of Scripture as their memories could bear. They were very early made to distinguish the Sabbath from other days, before they could well speak or go. They were as soon taught to be still at family prayers, and to ask a blessing immediately after, which they used to do by signs, before they could kneel or speak.

They were quickly made to understand they might have nothing they cried for, and instructed to speak handsomely for what they wanted. They were not suffered to ask even the lowest servant for aught without saying "Pray give me such a thing"; and the servant was chide if she ever let them omit that word.

Taking God's name in vain, cursing and swearing, profanity, obscenity, rude ill-bred names, were never heard among them; nor were they ever permitted to call each other by their proper names without the addition of brother or sister.

There was no such thing as loud playing or talking allowed of, but everyone was kept close to business to the six hours of school. And it is almost incredible what may be taught a child in a quarter of a year by a vigorous application, if it have but a tolerable capacity and good health. Kezzy excepted, all could read better in that time than the most of women can do as long as they live. Rising out of their places, or going out of the room, was not permitted except for good cause; and running into the yard, garden, or street, without leave, was always esteemed a capital offense.

For some years we went on very well. Never were children in better order. Never were children better disposed to piety, or in more subjection to their parents, till that fatal dispersion of them after the fire into several families. In these they were left at full liberty to converse with servants, which before they had always been restrained from , and to run abroad to play with any children, bad or good. They soon learned to neglect a strict observance of the Sabbath, and got knowledge of several songs and bad things which before they had no notion of. That civil behaviour which made them admired when they were at home, by all who saw them, was in a great measure lost, and a clownish accent and many rude ways were learnt which were not reformed without some difficulty.

When the house was rebuilt, and the children all brought home, we entered on a strict reform; and then was begun the system of singing psalms at the beginning and leaving school, morning and evening. Then also that of a general retirement at five o'clock was entered upon, when the eldest took the youngest that could speak,

and the second the next, to whom they read the psalms for the day
and a chapter in the New Testament; as in the morning they were
directed to read the psalms and a chapter in the Old Testament, after
which they went to their private prayers, before they got their
breakfast or came into the family.

There were observed several bye-laws among us. I mention them
here because I think them useful.

It had been observed that cowardice and fear of punishment
often lead children into lying till they get a custom of it which they
cannot leave. To prevent this, a law was made that whoever was
charged with a fault of which they were guilty, if they would ingenu-
ously confess it and promise to amend should not be beaten. This
rule prevented a great deal of lying, and would have done more if
one in the family would have observed it. But he could not be pre-
vailed upon, and therefore was often imposed on by false colours and
equivocations which none would have used but one, had they been
kindly dealt with; and some in spite of all would always speak truth
plainly.

That no sinful action, as lying, pilfering at church or on the
Lord's day, disobedience, quarreling, etc. should ever pass unpun-
ished.

That no child should be ever chided or beat twice for the same fault, and that if they amended they should never be upbraided with it afterwards.

That every signal act of obedience, especially when it crossed upon their own inclinations, should always be commended, and frequently rewarded according to the merits of the case.

That if ever any child performed an act of obedience, or did anything with intention to please, though the performance was not well, yet the obedience and intention should be kindly accepted, and the child with sweetness directed how to do better for the future.

That propriety be invariably preserved, and none suffered to invade the property of another in the smallest matter, though it were but of the value of a farthing or a pin, which they might not take from the owner without, much less against, his consent. This rule can never be too much inculcated on the minds of children; and from the want of parents or governors doing it as they ought, proceeds that shameful neglect of justice which we may observe in the world.

That promises be strictly observed; and a gift once bestowed, and so the right passed away from the donor, be not resumed, but left to the disposal of him to whom it was given, unless it were conditional, and the condition of the obligation not performed.

That no girl be taught to work till she can read very well; and that she be kept to her work with the same application and for the same time that she was held to in reading. This rule also is much to be observed, for the putting children to learn sewing before they can read perfectly is the very reason why so few women can read fit to be heard, and never to be well understood.

---

### KERMIT ROOSEVELT TO HIS BROTHER QUENTIN:
*American adventurer and son of Teddy Roosevelt, 1889–1943*

The great man never loses his child's heart. What is true of the Kingdom of God must also be true in the affairs of men.

# Courage

*There is little extraordinary about the achievements of a genius, a prodigy, or a savant. Inevitably, a great leader is someone who overcomes tremendous obstacles and still succeeds. That is the essence of courage. It is the ability to maintain, in the face of grave perils, a kind of incognizance of the consequences of doing right. It is the ability to maintain great strength without any impulsive compulsion to use it—that strength is to be held in reserve until and unless it becomes necessary to use it for the cause of right. Here several genuine heroes, courageous souls like the irrepressible American president Teddy Roosevelt, the Scottish adventurer and novelist Robert Lewis Stevenson, and the English founder of the Red Cross Florence Nightingale offer their insights into this singular character trait.*

## ROBERT LEWIS STEVENSON TO HIS EDITOR PATE HAMILTON:

*Scottish novelist and essayist, 1850–1894*

The world has no room for cowards. We must all be ready somehow to toil, to suffer, to die. And yours is not the less noble because no drum beats before you when you go out into your daily battlefields, and no crowds shout about your coming when you return from your daily victory or defeat.

---

## THEODORE ROOSEVELT TO HIS DAUGHTER ALICE:

*American author, adventurer, and president, 1858–1919*

Courage is not having the strength to go on; it is going on when you don't have the strength. Industry and determination can do anything that genius and advantage can do and many things that they cannot.

## Alvin York to his son Andrew:
*American World War I hero, 1887–1964*

The fear of God makes a hero; the fear of man makes a coward.

---

## John Buchan to his brother Walter:
*Scottish writer, governor-general of Canada, 1875–1940*

To see what is right and not to do it is cowardice. It is never a question of who is right but what is right.

# FLORENCE NIGHTINGALE TO PRIME MINISTER WILLIAM GLADSTONE:

*British nurse, 1820–1910*

Courage is a character trait most oft attributable to men. In fact, it is the universal virtue of all those who choose to do the right thing over the expedient thing. It is the common currency of all those who do what they are supposed to do in a time of conflict, crisis, and confusion.

In the Crimean War, courage was oft times more evident amongst the women and children, displaced by the fighting, ennobled by the devastation of their homes, who nevertheless determined to maintain their dignity, uphold their responsibilities, and undertake the rigors and ardors of ordinary life.

I am of certain convinced that the greatest heroes are those who do their duty in the daily grind of domestic affairs whilst the world whirls as a maddening dreidle.

# GEORGE GRANT TO HIS CHILDREN:

*American writer, 1954–*

History often has a way of surprising us. We will all undoubtedly be shocked to discover that most of the grand-glorious headline-making events of our day will actually go down in the annals of time as mere backdrops to the real drama of ordinary life—of fellow-workers, next-door neighbors, close friends, and family members. Despite all the hype, hoopla, and hysteria of sensational turns of events, the ordinary people who tend their gardens, raise their children, perfect their trades, and mind their businesses are, in the end more important. Just like they always have been. Just like they always will be.

That is one of the great lessons of history. It is simply that in the providence of God, ordinary people are ultimately the ones who determine the outcome of human events—not presidents and princes, not masters and tyrants. It is that laborers and workmen, cousins and acquaintances can upend the expectations of the brilliant and the glamorous, the expert and the meticulous. It is that plain folks, simple people, can literally change the course of history—because they are the stuff of which history is made. They are the ones who make the world go round. Sadly, that is an easy fact to forget.

But we can't forget it for long. The onward march of history won't let us. Suddenly we are awakened to it once again as babushkas with brooms and peasants with rakes topple fierce empires and redraw the very maps of the nations. Whether in Timisora or Tianaminn, in Moscow or Mobutu, in Boston or Biloxi, it is ordinary people who ultimately determine the destiny of nations. G.K. Chesterton once said: "The most extraordinary thing in the world is an ordinary man and an ordinary woman and their ordinary children. For indeed, the first shall be last and the last shall be first."

There is something extraordinary going on in our world today precisely because everyone on the stage of activity is so fiercely ordinary. As Chesterton pointed out, that irony, that paradox, that remarkable reversal, is woven into the very fabric of God's good providence in the world. Because some men cannot comprehend that, they condemn it; because they cannot understand it, they deny it. Beware lest that trap ensnare you. Recognize true character for what it is.

# *Death*

*To live well is a great achievement. But to die well is greater still—and it is far rarer. Though many will face the rigors of life with courage and gumption, few have the fortitude to so face death. The wise prepare their own hearts and that of their beloved for what is assuredly inevitable. Here sages as varied as the great contemporary evangelist Billy Graham, the twentieth-century French statesman Charles de Gaulle, the radical abolitionist John Brown, and the doomed queen of England Anne Boleyn offer their perspective on this most universal matter.*

# BILLY GRAHAM TO HIS SON FRANKLIN:

*American evangelist, 1918–*

We need to be reminded that there is nothing morbid about honestly confronting the fact of life's end, and preparing for it so that we may go gracefully and peacefully. It was the Psalmist, one of the world's wisest men who prayed, "So teach us to number our days, that we may apply our hearts unto wisdom." The fact is, we cannot truly face life until we have learned to face the fact that it will be taken away from us one day.

# CATO THE ELDER TO HIS SON:

*Roman statesman, 234–149 B.C.*

After I am dead I would rather have people ask why I have no monument than why I have one.

Sullivan Ballou, a Union soldier just before his death
at Bull Run, to his wife:

*Federal soldier, 1829–1861*

The indications are very strong that we shall move in a few days perhaps tomorrow and lest I should not be able to write you again I feel
impelled to write a few lines that may fall under your eye when I am
no more. Our movement may be one of a few days duration and be
full of pleasure. And it may be one of severe conflict and death to
me. "Not my will but thine O God be done" if it is necessary that I
should fall on the battle fiend [*sic.*] for my country I am ready. I have
no misgivings about or lack of confidence in the cause in which I am
engaged, and my courage does not halt or falter. I know how
American Civilization now leans upon the triumph of the
Government and how great a debt we owe to those who went before
us through the blood and suffering of the Revolution; and I am willing perfectly willing to lay down all my joys in this life to help maintain this government and to pay that debt.

But my dear wife when I know that with my own joys I lay down
nearly al [*sic.*] of yours, and replace them in this life with care and
sorrow when after having eaten for long years the bitter fruit of

orphanage myself. I must offer it as their only sustenance to my dear little children. Is it weak or dishonorable that while the banner of purpose flotes calmly and proudly in the breeze underneath my unbounded love for you my dear wife and children should struggle in fierce though useless contest with my love of country.

I cannot describe to you my feelings on this calm summer night when two thousand men are sleeping around me. Many of them enjoying the last perhaps before that of Death. And I suspicious that Death is creeping behind me with his fatal dart am communing with God my country and thee. I have sought most closely and diligently and often in my breast for a wrong motive in thus hazarding the happiness of all that I love and I could not find one. A pure love of my country and of the principles I have advocated before the people and the name of honour that I love more than I fear death have called upon me and I have obeyed.

Sarah my love for you is deathless it seems to bind me with mighty cables that nothing but Omnipotence can break and yet my love of country comes over me like a strong wind and bears me irresistably with all those chains to the battle field the memories of the blissful moments I have enjoyed with you come crowding over me. And I feel most deeply grateful to God and you that I have enjoyed them so long. And how hard it is for me to give them up! And burn to ashes the hopes of future years when God willing we might still have loved and loved together and see our boys grow up to honourable manhood around us. I know I have but few claims upon Divine Providence but something whispers to me perhaps it is the wafted prayer of my little Edgar that I shall return to my loved ones unharmed. If I do not my dear Sarah never forget how much I loved you nor that when my last breath escapes me on the battlefield it will whisper your name.

Forgive my many faults and the many pains I have caused you. How thoughtless how foolish I have sometimes been! How gladly would I wash out with my tears every little spot upon your happiness, and struggle with all the misfortunes of this world to shield you and my children from harm but I cannot. I must watch you from the spirit world and hover near you while you buffet the storms with your precious little freight—and wait with sad patience till we meet to part no more.

But Oh Sarah! If the dead can come back to this earth and flit unseen around those they love I shall be always with you in the brightest day and the darkest night amidst your happiest scenes and gloomiest hours—always, always—and when the soft breeze fans your cheek it shall be my breath or the cool air your throbbing temple it shall be my spirit passing by. Sarah do not mourn me dead think I am gone and wait for me for we shall meet again.

As for my little boys they will grow up as I have done and never know a father's love and care. Little Willie is too young to remember me long but my blue eyed Edgar will keep my frolics with him among the dimmest memories of his childhood

Sarah, I have unlimited confidence in your maternal care and your development of their characters. Tell my two mothers I call Gods blessings upon them Oh! Sarah I wait for you then come to me and lead thither my children.

---

## CHARLES DE GAULLE TO HIS FRIEND MADAME POMPIDOU:
*French general and politician, 1890–1970*

The graveyards are full of indispensable men.

## STONEWALL JACKSON TO HIS CHAPLAIN, ROBERT L. DABNEY:
*American Confederate general, 1824–1863*

I am not afraid to die. I am willing to abide by the will of my heavenly father. I know that heaven is in store for me, and I should rejoice in the prospect of going there tomorrow. But, still, I am ready to leave it any day for that heaven which I know awaits me I would not agree to the slightest diminution of one shade of my glory there, not for all the fame which I have acquired, or shall ever win in this world. Therefore I will be content and resigned to God's will.

---

## ANNE BOLEYN TO HER FATHER:
*Queen of England, second wife of Henry VIII, 1507–1536*

The executioner is, I hear, very expert, and my neck is very slender. I shall have little to fear then except fear itself.

# JOHN BROWN SAYS GOODBYE TO HIS FAMILY THE NIGHT BEFORE HE WAS EXECUTED:
### *American abolitionist, 1800–1859*

As I now begin what is probably the last letter I shall ever writ to any of you; I conclude to write you all at the same time. I am waiting the hour of my public murder with great composure of mind, and cheerfulness: feeling the strongest assurance that in no other possible way could I be used to so much advance the cause of God; and of humanity: and that nothing that either I or all my family have sacrificed or suffered: will be lost.

The reflection that a wise and merciful, as well as just & holy God: rules not only the affairs of this world; but of all worlds; is a rock to set our feet upon; under all circumstances: even those more severely trying ones: into which our own follies; and wrongs have placed us. I have now no doubt but that our seeming disaster: will ultimately result in the most glorious success. So my dear shattered and broken family be of good cheer and believe and trust in God; "with all your heart and with all your soul;" for "he doeth All things well." Do not feel ashamed on my account; nor for one moment despair of the cause; or grow weary of well doing. I bless God; I never felt stronger confidence in the certain and near approach of a bright Morning; and a glorious day; than I have felt; and do now feel; since my confinement here.

I am endeavoring to "return" like a "poor Prodigal" as I am, to my Father: against whom I have always sinned: in the hope; that he may kindly, & forgivingly "meet me: though a very great way off." Oh my dear Wife and Children would "to God" you could know how I have been "traveling in birth for you" all: that no one of you "may fail of the grace of God, through Jesus Christ:" that no one of you may be blind to the truth: and glorious "light of his word," in which Life; and Immortality; are brought to light.

I beseech you every one to make the bible your daily and Nightly study; with a childlike honest, candid, teachable spirit: out of love and respect for your husband; and Father: and I beseech the God of my Fathers; to open all your eyes to a discovery of the truth. You cannot imagine how much you may son [*sic.*] need the consolations of the Christian religion.

Circumstances like my own; for more than a month past; convince beyond all doubt: of our great need: of something more to rest our hopes on; than merely our own vague theories framed up, while our prejudices are excited; or our vanity worked up to its highest pitch.

Oh do not trust your eternal all upon the boisterous Ocean, without even a Helm; or Compass to aid you in steering. I do not ask any of you; to throw away your reason: I only ask you, to make a candid and sober use of your reason: My dear younger children will you listen to the last poor admonition of one who can only love you? Oh be determined at once to give your whole hearts to God; and let nothing shake; or alter; that resolution. You need have no fear of regretting it.

Do not be vain, and thoughtless: but sober minded. And let me entreat you all to love the whole remnant of our once great family: "with a pure heart fervently." Try to build again: your broken walls: and to make the utmost of every stone that is left. Nothing can so tend to make life a blessing as the consciousness that you love: and are beloved: and "love ye the stranger" still. It is ground of the utmost comfort to my mind: to know that so many of you as have had the opportunity; have given full proof of your fidelity to the great family of man.

Be faithful until death. From the exercise of habitual love to man: it cannot be very hard: to learn to love his maker. I must yet insert a resin for my firm belief in the Divine inspiration of the Bible: notwithstanding I am (perhaps naturally) skeptical: (certainly not, credulous). I wish you all to consider it most thoroughly; when you read the blessed book; and see whether you can not discover such evidence yourselves. It is the purity of heart, feeling, or motive: as well as word, and action which is everywhere insisted on; that distinguish it from all other teachings; that commends it to my conscience; whether my heart be "willing, and obedient" or not. The inducements that it holds out; are another reason of my conviction of its truth: and genuineness: that I cannot here omit; in this my last argument for the Bible.

Eternal life; is that my soul is "panting after" this moment. I mention this; as reason for endeavoring to leave a valuable copy of the Bible to be carefully preserved in remembrance of me: to so many of my posterity; instead of some other things of equal cost.

I beseech you all to live in habitual contentment with very moderate circumstances: and gains, of worldly store: and most earnestly to teach this: to your children; and Children's Children; after you: by example: as well; as precept. Be determined to know by experience as soon as may be: whether bible instruction is of Divine origin or not; which says; "Owe no man anything but to love one another." John Rogers writes to his children to abhor with undying hatred, also: that "sum of all villainies;" Slavery.

Remember that "he that is slow to anger is better than the mighty: and he that ruleth his spirit; than he that taketh a city,"

Remember also: that "they that be wise shall shine; and they that turn many to righteousness: as the stars forever; and ever." And now dearly beloved Farewell, To God and the word of his grace I commend you all.

# *Education*

*$A$ll talk of education should be for us a reminder that we have only just begun to learn how to learn. It is an affirmation that though our magnificent heritage has introduced us to the splendid wonders of literature and art and music and history and science and ideas in the past—we have only just been introduced and that a lifetime adventure in these vast and portentous arenas still awaits us. Indeed, the most valuable lessons that education can convey are invariably the lessons that never end. Here great men and great minds all agree—from the Christian saints Paul and Augustine to the Reforming stalwarts Isaac Watts and John Buchan, among others—on the vital import of this never ending quest for enlightenment and self-improvement.*

### SIR WALTER SCOTT TO HIS SON CHARLES:
*Scottish poet and novelist, 1771–1832*

Though some people may have scrambled into distinction without a perfect knowledge of the classical languages, it is always with the greatest difficulty, like climbing over a wall instead of giving your ticket at the door.

---

### NATHAN BEDFORD FORREST TO HIS SON WILLIAM:
*American Confederate general, 1821–1877*

No one knows the embarrassment I labor under when thrown in the company of educated persons.

---

### DEREK BORK TO HIS YOUNG COUSIN:
*American educator and critic, 1891–1970*

If you think education is expensive, try ignorance.

# G.K. Chesterton to his brother Cecil:

*❧ English poet, novelist, and essayist, 1874–1936 ❧*

The great intellectual tradition that comes down to us from the past was never interrupted or lost through such trifles as the sack of Rome, the triumph of Attila, or all the barbarian invasions of the Dark Ages. It was lost after the introduction of printing, the discovery of America, the coming of the marvels of technology, the establishment of universal education, and all the enlightenment of the modern world. It was there, if anywhere, that there was lost or impatiently snapped the long thin delicate thread that had descended from distant antiquity; the thread of that unusual human hobby: the habit of thinking.

---

# St. Augustine to a young disciple:

*❧ Christian patriarch and philosopher, Bishop of Hippo, 354–430 ❧*

Education is the food of youth, the delight of old age, the ornament of prosperity, the refuge and comfort of adversity, and the provocation to grace in the soul.

# FRANCIS BACON TO A CATHEDRAL SCHOOL PRIOR:

*English philosopher, essayist, courtier, jurist, and statesman, 1561–1626*

History makes men wise; poetry, witty; mathematics, subtle; natural philosophy, deep; literature, grave; logic and rhetoric, able to contend; theology, humble; and each of these taken together makes men a true education of moral philosophy.

---

# ISAAC WATTS TO HIS NEPHEW:

*English poet, theologian, and hymn-writer, 1674–1748*

Suffer not any beloved study to prejudice your mind so far in favor of it as to despise all other learning. This is a fault of some little souls who have got a smattering of astronomy, metaphysics, history, or music and for want of due acquaintance with other arts, make a scoff at them all in comparison with their favorite.

JOHN BUCHAN TO THE CANADIAN EDUCATOR JAMES GRANT:
*Scottish writer, governor-general of Canada, 1875–1940*

Our greatest inheritance, the very foundation of our civilization, is a marvel to behold and consider. If I tried to describe its rich legacy with utmost brevity, I should take the Latin word humanitas. It represents in the widest sense, the accumulated harvest of the ages, the fine flower of a long discipline of Christian thought. It is the Western mind of which we ought to turn our attentions to careful study.

The now frivolously disregarded *Trivium*—emphasizing the basic classical scholastic categories of grammar, logic, and rhetoric—once equipped untold generations of young pupils with the essential tack and apparatus for a lifetime of learning. These are the very notions that once set acourse the great cultural flowering of Christendom over the past thousand years.

Indeed, this sort of educational philosophy and methodology is that which steadfastly affirms that every student, every family, every community, and every nation needs to be grounded in the good things, the great things, the true things in order to do the right things.

## THE APOSTLE PAUL TO THE CHRISTIANS IN THE CITY OF CORINTH:

*Christian apostle and missionary, c. 10–65*

For whatsoever things were written aforetime were written for our learnings.

---

## DANIEL WYTTENBACH TO HIS DAUGHTER:

*American literary critic and syndicated columnist, 1891–1963*

There is no business, no avocation whatsoever, which will not permit a man who has the inclination, to give a little time, every day, to study.

---

## SACHA GUITRY TO DOROTHY PARKER:

*American author and celebrated wit, 1893–1967*

You can pretend to be serious or grave; you can't pretend to be witty or wise.

# *Faith*

*Without faith it is impossible to please God. Similarly, without faith it is impossible to please man, it is impossible to satisfy ourselves, and it is impossible to build lasting cultural standards, institutions, and values. Faith is literally the glue that holds together the harried elements of life. Here correspondents like the Apostle Paul, the English twentieth-century journalist Hilaire Belloc, King George VI, and the American inspirational writer Elizabeth Prentiss all probe faith's vital essence.*

# HILAIRE BELLOC TO HIS DEAR FRIEND MRS. RAYMOND ASQUITH:

*English poet, historian, and critic, 1870–1953*

I have, all these days, been thinking of a phrase which you use and which I have used in speaking with you: I mean the phrase that "suffering benefits (can benefit) the soul." You said—no more than it does the body. A sharp reminder may benefit the body and the mind too—but not torture. And the suffering of which we spoke was that profound thing which imperils: the apparent invitation to despair. And you said that such suffering could not but injure the soul, but I said it would (and should) benefit the soul.

Now that saying might be read as nonsense—contradiction in terms—or as what is worse than nonsense by far—I mean it might be read as one of those falsehoods whereby men drug themselves: the falsehoods which pass under the name of religion and cut off, in their swarm and buzzing through the modern world, the sight of religion and the understanding of final philosophy. It might be read as one of those drugs of illusion which are the most despicable of puerilities and weaknesses. But it is not that. The worst of suffering can and should confirm the soul at last: for this reason: that it is of time, and the soul is, ultimately, on another plane.

You know that I express badly. I was never meant to use words. I only took to it as a trade when the failure at Oxford [his failure to win a fellowship at All Souls] compelled me to take to writing as a living. I have the greatest difficulty in putting ultimate things with exactitude. It means parallel and metaphor, and parallel and metaphor are not in my métier. But I will attempt it here, because the matter is of such importance. It is of vital importance. It is the only really important thing in the world, this understanding of Life and Death.

When one says "The Soul" one does not mean a mood, a state of mind. These are indeed functions of the soul. But here (if indeed the soul—the principle of life and personality—be immortal, as it is) such things are of their nature a function of time: only, the permanent thing by which we are ("we are" does not mean only "we continue to be", it means "we continue to be ourselves"—it is "we" as well as "are"), are form and substance. Here the moods, the state of mind, a function of the soul, is also a function of time. But "here" is the life of this world. Now behind all that, and completing it, is the permanent life of the soul, and to that suffering can be used.

See how true it is, in experience, that this permanence of the Soul is. What is responsibility? Why are we ashamed 20 years after—or a day after for that matter—of real weakness or wrong doing? Why are we loyal, we human beings: why do we know that loyalty is fruitful (as we do), why are we convinced of the necessity of sacrifice and why do we admire it in all and in others—and even (if we are just to ourselves) in ourselves? It is because the Soul is conscious of its immortal habitation. Plato thought it "remembered" the divine. He was wrong. But the instinct is certainly communicated. How otherwise are the great emotions utterly different from the lesser? How otherwise are we sure (and we are sure) that they are of a quite separate quality, indefinitely, incommensurably, superior to the rest: as much as music is superior to clichés of talk, of sight and touch to vague memories, or the recognition of a person to the mere catalogue of qualities, or the thing to the name?

True, the beatitude which can be earned and deserved, is a mood: but a mood secure and infinite in character and unchangeable: rest and action in one. Here mood means something else: something much less. When it is happy it is a promise of beatitude, when it is unhappy it is either a warning of what the loss of beatitude would be, or (and) a task, an imposition, a burden—to be performed, accomplished, born. And the bearing of it is a fruitful thing.

Martyrdom means witness. We are not the creatures of change and loss but their victims for a time and our right protest is to tell them that they are inferior altogether to our very selves.

> "Not time, nor memory, not good fortune, no
> Not all the weight of all the wears of the world."

The alternative to this doctrine is, for noble minds, despair, and for the ignoble, puerilities. Neither are true. Despair is false because the universe is one: it is an equation with roots, not a mere pluralism and chaos. Puerilities stand self-condemned.

The truth is in neither. It is in the mystery, consonant to instinct and experience, that time and shame and their aspect of loss are in a system subject to, ambassadorial to, introduction to, the full end—by which and for which we are. Therein we recover. And the picture which the poor and humble make of reunion and of pleasant places is right. They shall be filled. Only—like a child hearing of grown-up life—it will be more than they thought.

What I mean is, be secure. As one says in a hard passage oversea by night—be certain that evils as well as the lesser goods have an end, and that with a right endurance the greater goods are recovering, or rather reached again.

# ELIZABETH PRENTISS TO A YOUNG FRIEND:

*American novelist and hymnwriter, 1818–1878*

You ask if I "ever feel that religion is a sham?" No, never. I know it is a reality. If you ask if I am ever staggered by the inconsistencies of professing Christians, I say yes, I am often made heartsick by them; but heartsickness always makes me run to Christ, and one good look at Him pacifies me. This is in fact my panacea for every ill; and as to my own sinfulness, that would certainly overwhelm me if I spent much time in looking at it. But it is a monster whose face I do not love to see; I turn from its hideousness to the beauty of His face who sins not, and the sight of "yon lovely Man" ravishes me. But at your age I did this only by fits and starts, and suffered as you do. So I know how to feel for you, and what to ask for you. God purposely sickens us of man and of self, that we may learn to "look long at Jesus."

# KING GEORGE VI TO MINNIE HASKINS:

*◦{ King of Great Britain and Northern Ireland, emperor of India, 1895–1952 }◦*

I said to a man who stood at the gate of the year: "Give me a light that I may tread safely into the unknown." And he replied: "Go out into the darkness and put your hand into the hand of God. That shall be to you better than a light and safer than a known way." And indeed it is.

---

# THE APOSTLE PAUL TO HIS YOUNG FRIEND TIMOTHY:

*◦{ Christian apostle and missionary, c. 10–65 }◦*

I have fought the good fight of faith.

*One* ne needn't be a gourmet cook or a renowned chef to comprehend the vital importance of good food in all our lives. It is not merely fuel for our bodies. Instead it is refreshment for our souls. It is the hub upon which fellowship turns. It is the catalyst for friendship. Indeed, it is art and craft and sustenance and recreation and social medium all rolled together. Here several experts—like chef James Beard and gourmand Bernard Levin—and several non-experts—like contemporary author George Grant and etiquette expert Judith Martin—all take a shot at explaining this culinary and cultural phenomenon.*

### JAMES BEARD TO JUDITH MARTIN:
*American cookery expert, 1903–1985*

The secret of cooking is first, having a love of it. If you're convinced cooking is drudgery, you're never going to be any good at it, and you might as well just warm up something frozen.

---

### JUDITH MARTIN TO JAMES BEARD:
*American author and etiquette expert, 1946–*

I concur with your assessment of drudgery in the kitchen with but one caveat: never, never should one eat anything out of a carton, if one is at home alone with the shades drawn. Doing so is wicked and constitutes Miss Manners' one exception to the generally genial rule about violations of etiquette not counting if you don't get caught.

## GEORGE GRANT TO HIS WIFE KAREN:

*American writer, 1954–*

"The way to a man's heart is his stomach," said the inimitable Samuel Johnson. "Similarly, the way to a man's theology is the setting of his table at the various seasonal celebrations." Indeed, there is little that is more revealing of our ultimate concerns than what we eat and how we eat it.

Generally we moderns tend to think of faith as a rather other-worldly concern while we think of food as a rather this-worldly concern. It is difficult for us to see how the twain could ever meet. In fact though, food and faith are inextricably linked. And while that is true to one degree or another in every culture the world over, it is especially evident in the Judeo-Christian tradition of the West.

Interestingly, the word faith is used less than 300 times in the Bible while the verb to eat is used more than 800 times. You can hardly read a single page of the Scriptures without running into a discussion of bread and wine, of milk and honey, of leeks and onions, of glistening oil and plump figs, sweet grapes and delectable pomegranates, of roast lamb and savory stew. Throughout there are images of feasts and celebrations. The themes of justice and virtue are often defined in terms of food while the themes of hungering and thirsting are inevitably defined in terms of faith. Community and hospitality are evidences of a faithful covenant while righteousness and holiness are evidences of a healthy appetite. Biblical worship—in both the Old and the New Testaments—does not revolve around some esoteric discussion of philosophy or some ascetic ritual enactment, but around a Meal.

As if to underscore this, all of the resurrection appearances of Christ occurred at meals—with the single exception of the garden tomb. On the road to Emmaus, in the Upper Room, and at the edge of the Sea of Galilee, Jesus supped with His disciples. Indeed, He did not say, "Behold, I stand at the door and knock. If anyone opens the door, I will enter in and discuss theology with him." No. Jesus said, "I will come in and sup with him."

Food is the stuff of life. And the Christian faith reminds us that Jesus came to give us life—indeed, He came to give us "abundant life." So, it is not surprising for Him—as well as all of the apostles and prophets—to utilize food as a primary image in the conveyance of the Christian worldview.

When the subject of worldview comes up, we generally think of philosophy—not cooking. And that is really too bad. We think of intellectual niggling. We think of the brief and blinding oblivion of ivory tower speculation, of thickly obscure tomes, and of inscrutable logical complexities.

In fact, a worldview is as practical as potatoes. It is less metaphysical than understanding marginal market buying at the stock exchange or legislative initiatives in Congress. It is less esoteric than typing a book into a laptop computer or sending a fax across the continent. It is instead as down to earth as grinding condiments for a savory sauce.

The word itself is a poor English attempt at translating the German weltanshauung. It literally means a "life perspective" or "a way of seeing." It is simply the way we look at the world. You have a worldview. I have a worldview. Everyone does. It is our perspective. It is our frame of reference. It is the means by which we interpret the situations and circumstances around us. It is what enables us to integrate all the different aspects of our faith, and life, and experience.

And the Christian view of the world is fraught with a sort of cook's paradox—an appreciation for both the potentialities and the liabilities of fallen creation. The problem is that we tend to want to hammer out our philosophy of life in isolation from life. We disconnect our worldview from the world. We either become so heavenly minded that we're no earthly good or we become so earthly minded that we're no heavenly good. The Christian tradition on the other hand, affords us a distinctively balanced worldview that encourages us to be "in the world" but not be entirely "of it."

The reason for this seemingly contradictory state of affairs—a kind of enmity with the world on the one hand and a responsibility to it on the other—is simply that "God so loved the world that He gave His only begotten Son." Though the world is "in the power of the evil one" and "knows not God, neither the children of God," He is "reconciling the world unto Himself."

A genuinely integrated Biblical worldview must be cognizant of this remarkable sort of cook's paradox. It must be engaged in the world. It must be unengaged in worldliness. It must somehow correlate spiritual concerns with temporal concerns. It must coalesce heavenly hope and landed life. It must coordinate heart-felt faith and down-to-earth practice.

That is a difficult ideal to visualize—much less to implement in our lives. But that is just what a healthy apprehension of the connection between food and faith enables us to do. By vitally connecting the head with the hand with the heart with the palate, by placing emphasis on the whole of life—our relationships, traditions, simple joys, family celebrations, tastes, pleasures, and expressions of thanksgiving—the high ideals of a Biblical worldview are happily instituted in the very warp and woof of our existence. Perhaps that is why God so clearly portrays the essence of the New Covenant in a Meal. His aim appears rather simple: His gracious provision is to utterly invade what we are and what we do, what we think and how we act, and what we believe and what we eat.

According to Samuel Johnson, that covenantal link is ultimately inescapable. Looking across the wide span of Christ's covenantal activity, it is obvious that he was right. Isn't it amazing how easily we overlook the obvious? "Taste and see that the Lord, He is good" (Psalm 34:8).

# Bernard Levinson to his nephew:

*American journalist, 1866–1939*

"Bless thy good creatures to our use, and us to thy table." This was the grace before meals at my school, and it seems to me to sum up admirably a truly balanced attitude to the pleasures of food and drink. We must keep these pleasures in proper perspective; we must indulge them reasonably, not grossly. The savor of good food and drink is one of the elements of true civilization, and no man who embarks upon a fine meal in that knowledge can rise from it without thinking something real has been added to his nature.

# *Forgiveness*

*In this poor fallen world none of us has gone a day without the need for forgiveness. We need forgiveness for our sins of omission and commission alike. We need forgiveness for our slights and blunders, for our insults and mistakes, for our incognizance and our improvidence. But we need to forgive just as much as we need to be forgiven. Here John Milton the great seventeenth century English poet, Corrie ten Boom the Dutch saint who saved Jews from the Nazis, and Herman Melville the astonishingly gifted author of Moby Dick and other classics illumine this vital matter.*

# JOHN MILTON TO HIS WIFE:
*English poet and scholar, 1608–1674*

Let us no more contend, nor blame each other, blamed enough elsewhere, but strive in offices of love, how we may lighten each other's burden, in our share of woe.

---

# MARTIN LUTHER KING, JR. TO CALEB SMITH:
*American cleric and civil rights leader, 1929–1968*

We must develop and maintain the capacity to forgive. He who is devoid of the power to forgive is devoid of the power to love. There is some good in the worst of us and some evil in the best of us. When we discover this, we are less prone to hate our enemies.

# CORRIE TEN BOOM TO THE MAN WHO BETRAYED HER FAMILY TO THE NAZIS:

*◦┤ Dutch author and missionary, 1892–1983 ├◦*

Today I heard that most probably you are the one who betrayed me. I went through 10 months of concentration camp. My father died after 9 days of imprisonment. My sister died in prison, too.

The harm you planned was turned into good for me by God. I came nearer to Him. A severe punishment is awaiting you. I have prayed for you, that the Lord may accept you if you will repent. Think that the Lord Jesus on the Cross also took your sins upon Himself. If you accept this and want to be His child, you are saved for Eternity.

I have forgiven you everything. God will also forgive you everything, if you ask Him. He loves you and He Himself sent His Son to earth to reconcile your sins, which meant to suffer the punishment for you and me. You, on your part have to give an answer to this. If He says: "Come unto Me, give Me your heart," then your answer must be: "Yes, Lord, I come, make me your child." If it is difficult for you to pray, then ask if God will give you His Spirit, who works the faith in your heart.

Never doubt the Lord Jesus' love. He is standing with His arms spread out to receive you. I hope that the path which you will now take may work for your eternal salvation.

---

## Herman Melville to his daughter:
*⊶ American adventurer and novelist, 1819–1891 ⊷*

Give not thyself up, then, to fire, lest it invert thee, deaden thee; as for a time it did me. There is a wisdom that is woe; but there is a woe that is madness. And there is a Catskill eagle in some souls that can alike dive down into the blackest gorges, and soar out of them again and become invisible in the sunny places. And even if he forever flies within the gorge, that gorge is in the mountains; so that even in his lowest swoop the mountain eagle is still higher than other birds upon the plain, even though they soar. Such high-mindedness begins at the point of forgiveness.

# *Freedom*

*The* great cry of every human heart is for freedom. Regardless of the time, the culture, or the political climate, the desire for liberty is woven into the fabric of every man's heart. Perhaps that is why the long history of tyranny is so galling to us. Here the great eighteenth-century critic and lexicographer Samuel Johnson joins his voice with that of civil rights pioneer Martin Luther King Jr. in pronouncing its principles and elucidating its precepts.

# SAMUEL JOHNSON ARGUING IN FAVOR OF A SLAVE CLAIMING HIS LIBERTY IN THE SCOTTISH COURTS:

*English writer and lexicographer, 1709–1784*

It must be agreed that in most ages many countries have had part of their inhabitants in a state of slavery; yet it may be doubted whether slavery can ever be supposed the natural condition of man. It is impossible not to conceive that men in their original state were equal; and very difficult to imagine how one would be subjected to another but by violent compulsion.

An individual may, indeed, forfeit his liberty by a crime; but he cannot by that crime forfeit the liberty of his children. What is true of a criminal seems true likewise of a captive. A man may accept life from a conquering enemy on condition of perpetual servitude; but it is very doubtful whether he can entail that servitude on his descendants; for no man can stipulate without commission for another. The condition which he himself accepts, his son or grandson perhaps would have rejected.

If we should admit, what perhaps may with more reason be denied, that there are certain relations between man and man which may make slavery necessary and just, yet it can never be proved that he who is now suing for his freedom ever stood in any of those relations. He is certainly subject by no law, but that of violence, to his present master; who pretends no claim to his obedience, but that he bought him from a merchant of slaves, whose right to sell him was never examined.

It is said that according to the constitutions of Jamaica he was legally enslaved; these constitutions are merely positive; and apparently injurious to the rights of mankind, because whoever is exposed to sale is condemned to slavery without appeal; by whatever fraud or violence he might have been originally brought into the merchant's power. In our own time princes have been sold, by wretches to whose care they were entrusted, that they might have a European education; but when once they were brought to a market in the plantations, little would avail either their dignity or their wrongs. The laws of Jamaica afford a negro no redress. His color is considered as a sufficient testimony against him. It is to be lamented that moral right on one side, and no convenience on the other.

Inhabitants of this island can neither gain riches nor power by taking away the liberty of any part of the human species. The sum of the argument is this: No man is by nature the property of another: The defendant is, therefore, by nature free: The rights of nature must be some way forfeited before they can be justly taken away. That the defendant has by any act forfeited the rights of nature we require to be proved; and if no proof of such forfeiture can be given, we doubt not but the justice of the court will declare him free.

---

## Harry Emerson Fosdick to Henry Van Dyke:

*American author and pastor, 1878–1969*

America is a passionate belief in freedom and in the worth and dignity of the human personality. We must not let the song die on our lips.

# MARTIN LUTHER KING, JR. TO HIS BRETHREN IN THE CLERGY:

*American cleric and civil rights leader, 1929–1968*

While confined here in the Birmingham City Jail, I came across your recent statement calling our present activities "unwise and untimely." Since I feel that you are men of genuine goodwill and your criticisms are sincerely set forth, I would like to answer your statement in what I hope will be patient and reasonable terms.

I think I should give the reason for my being in Birmingham, since you have been influenced by the argument of "outsiders coming in." Several months ago our local affiliate here in Birmingham invited us to be on call to engage in a nonviolent direct action program if such were deemed necessary. So I am here, along with several members of my staff, because we were invited here. I am here because I have basic organizational ties here.

Beyond this, I am in Birmingham because injustice is here. Just as the eighth-century prophets left their little villages and carried their "thus saith the Lord" far beyond the boundaries of their home towns; and just as the Apostle Paul left his little village of Tarsus and carried the gospel of Jesus Christ to practically every hamlet and city of the Graeco-Roman world, I too am compelled to carry the gospel of freedom beyond my particular home town. Like Paul, I must constantly respond to the Macedonian call for aid.

Moreover, I am cognizant of the interrelatedness of all communities and states. I cannot sit idly by in Atlanta and not be concerned about what happens in Birmingham. Injustice anywhere is a threat to justice everywhere. We are caught in an inescapable network of mutuality, tied in a single garment of destiny. Whatever affects one directly affects all indirectly. Never again can we afford to live with the narrow, provincial "outside agitator" idea. Anyone who lives inside the United States can never be considered an outsider anywhere in this country.

You deplore the demonstrations that are presently taking place in Birmingham. But I am sorry that your statement did not express a similar concern for the conditions that brought the demonstrations into being. I am sure that each of you would want to go beyond the superficial social analyst who looks merely at effects, and does not grapple with underlying causes. I would not hesitate to say that it is unfortunate that so called demonstrations are taking place in Birmingham at this time, but I would say in more emphatic terms that it is even more unfortunate that the white power structure of this city left the Negro community with no other alternative.

Birmingham is probably the most thoroughly segregated city in the United States. Its ugly record of police brutality is known in every section of this country. Its unjust treatment of Negroes in the courts is a notorious reality. There have been more unsolved bombings of Negro homes and churches in Birmingham than in any city in this nation. These are the hard, brutal, and unbelievable facts. On the basis of these conditions Negro leaders sought to negotiate with the city fathers. But the political leaders consistently refused to engage in good-faith negotiation.

You may well ask, "Why direct action? Why sit-ins, marches, etceteras? Isn't negotiation a better path?" You are exactly right in your call for negotiation. Indeed, this is the purpose of direct action. Nonviolent direct action seeks to create such a crisis and establish such creative tension that a community that has constantly refused to negotiate is forced to confront the issue. It seeks so to dramatize the issue that it can no longer be ignored. I just referred to the creation of tension as a part of the work of the nonviolent resister. This may sound rather shocking. But I must confess that I am not afraid of the word tension. I have earnestly worked and preached against violent tension, but there is a type of constructive nonviolent tension that is necessary for growth. Just as Socrates felt that it was necessary to create a tension in the mind so that individuals could rise from the bondage of myths and half-truths to the unfettered realm of creative analysis and objective appraisal, we must see the need of having nonviolent gadflies to create the kind of tension in society that will help men to rise from the dark depths of prejudice and racism to the majestic heights of understanding and brotherhood. So the purpose of the direct action is to create a situation so crisis-packed that it will inevitably open the door to negotiation. We, therefore, concur with you in your call for negotiation. Too long has our beloved Southland been bogged down in the tragic attempt to live in monologue rather than dialogue.

My friends, I must say to you that we have not made a single gain in civil rights without determined legal and nonviolent pressure. History is the long and tragic story of the fact that privileged groups seldom give up their privileges voluntarily. Individuals may see the moral light and voluntarily give up their unjust posture; but as Reinhold Neibuhr has reminded us, groups are more immoral than individuals.

We know through painful experience that freedom is never voluntarily given by the oppressor; it must be demanded by the oppressed. Frankly, I have never yet engaged in a direct-action movement that was "well timed," according to the timetable of those who have not suffered unduly from the disease of segregation. For years now I have heard the word "Wait!" It rings in the ear of every Negro with a piercing familiarity. This "wait" has almost always meant "never." It has been a tranquilizing thalidomide, relieving the emotional stress for a moment, only to give birth to an ill-formed infant of frustration. We must come to see with the distinguished jurist of yesterday that "justice too long delayed is justice denied." We have waited for more than three hundred and forty years for our constitutional and God-given rights. The nations of Asia and Africa are moving with jet-like speed toward the goal of political independence, and we still creep at horse and buggy pace toward the gaining of a cup of coffee at a lunch counter. I guess it is easy for those who have never felt the stinging darts of segregation to say, "Wait." But when you have seen vicious mobs lynch your mothers and fathers at will and drown your sisters and brothers at whim, when you have seen hate-filled policemen curse, kick, brutalize, and even kill your black brothers and sisters with impunity; when you see the vast majority of your twenty million Negro brothers smothering in an airtight cage of poverty in the midst of an affluent society; when you suddenly find your tongue twisted and your speech stammering as you seek to explain to your six-year-old daughter why she can't go to the public amusement park that has just been advertised on television, and see tears welling up in her little eyes when she is told that

Funtown is closed to colored children, and see the depressing clouds
of inferiority begin to form in her little mental sky, and see her
begin to distort her little personality by unconsciously developing a
bitterness toward white people; when you have to concoct an answer
for a five-year-old son asking in agonizing pathos: "Daddy, why do
white people treat colored people so mean?"; when you take a cross
country drive and find it necessary to sleep night after night in the
uncomfortable corners of your automobile because no motel will
accept you, when you are humiliated day in and day out by nagging
signs reading "white" and "colored"; when your first name becomes
"nigger" and your middle name becomes "boy" (however old you
are) and your last name becomes "John," and when your wife and
mother are never given the respected title "Mrs."; when you are harried by day and haunted at night by the fact that you are a Negro,
living constantly at tip-toe stance never quite knowing what to
expect next, and plagued with inner fears and outer resentments;
when you are forever fighting a degenerating sense of "nobodiness";
then you will understand why we find it difficult to wait. There
comes a time when the cup of endurance runs over, and men are no
longer willing to be plunged into an abyss of injustice where they
experience the blackness of corroding despair. I hope, sirs, you can
understand our legitimate and unavoidable impatience.

You express a great deal of anxiety over our willingness to break laws. This is certainly a legitimate concern. Since we so diligently urge people to obey the Supreme Court's decision of 1954 outlawing segregation in the public schools, it is rather strange and paradoxical to find us consciously breaking laws. One may well ask, "How can you advocate breaking some laws and obeying others?" The answer is found in the fact that there are two types of laws: There are just and there are unjust laws. I would agree with Saint Augustine that "an unjust law is no law at all."

Now what is the difference between the two? How does one determine when a law is just or unjust? A just law is a man-made code that squares with the moral law or the law of God. An unjust law is a code that is out of harmony with the moral law. To put it in the terms of Saint Thomas Aquinas, an unjust law is a human law that is not rooted in eternal and natural law. Any law that uplifts human personality is just. Any law that degrades human personality is unjust. All segregation statutes are unjust because segregation distorts the soul and damages the personality. It gives the segregator a false sense of superiority, and the segregated a false sense of inferiority. To use the words of Martin Buber, the great Jewish philosopher, segregation substitutes an "I-it" relationship for the "I-thou" relationship, and ends up relegating persons to the status of things. So segregation is not only politically, economically, and sociologically unsound, but it is morally wrong and sinful. Paul Tillich has said that sin is separation. Isn't segregation an existential expression of man's tragic separation, an expression of his awful estrangement, his terrible sinfulness? So I can urge men to disobey segregation ordinances because they are morally wrong.

There are some instances when a law is just on its face and unjust in its application. For instance, I was arrested Friday on a charge of parading without a permit. Now there is nothing wrong with an ordinance which requires a permit for a parade, but when the ordinance is used to preserve segregation and to deny citizens the First Amendment privilege of peaceful assembly and peaceful protest, then it becomes unjust.

I hope you can see the distinction I am trying to point out. In no sense do I advocate evading or defying the law as the rabid segregationist would do. This would lead to anarchy. One who breaks an unjust law must do it openly, lovingly (not hatefully as the white mothers did in New Orleans when they were seen on television screaming "nigger, nigger, nigger"), and with a willingness to accept the penalty. I submit that an individual who breaks a law that conscience tells him is unjust, and willingly accepts the penalty by staying in jail to arouse the conscience of the community over its injustice, is in reality expressing the very highest respect for law.

Of course, there is nothing new about this kind of civil disobedience. It was seen sublimely in the refusal of Shadrach, Meshach, and Abednego to obey the laws of Nebuchadnezzar because a higher moral law was involved. It was practiced superbly by the early Christians who were willing to face hungry lions and the excruciating pain of chopping blocks, before submitting to certain unjust laws of the Roman empire. To a degree academic freedom is a reality today because Socrates practiced civil disobedience.

We can never forget that everything Hitler did in Germany was "legal" and everything the Hungarian freedom fighters did in Hungary was "illegal." It was "illegal" to aid and comfort a Jew in Hitler's Germany. But I am sure that if I had lived in Germany during that time, I would have aided and comforted my Jewish brothers even though it was illegal. If I lived in a Communist country today, where certain principles dear to the Christian faith are suppressed, I believe I would openly advocate disobeying these anti-religious laws. I must make two honest confessions to you, my Christian and Jewish brothers. First, I must confess that over the last few years I have been gravely disappointed with the white moderate. I have almost reached the regrettable conclusion that the Negro's great stumbling block in the stride toward freedom is not the White Citizen's Councilor or the Ku Klux Klanner, but the white moderate who is more devoted to "order" than to justice; who prefers a negative peace which is the absence of tension to a positive peace which is the presence of justice; who constantly says "I agree with you in the goal you seek, but I can't agree with your methods of direct action"; who paternalistically feels that he can set the timetable for another man's freedom; who lives by the myth of time and who constantly advises the Negro to wait until a "more convenient season." Shallow understanding from people of goodwill is more frustrating than absolute misunderstanding from people of ill will. Lukewarm acceptance is much more bewildering than outright rejection.

I had hoped that the white moderate would understand that law and order exist for the purpose of establishing justice, and that when they fail to do this they become dangerously structured dams that block the flow of social progress. I had hoped that the white moderate would understand that the present tension in the South is merely a necessary phase of the transition from an obnoxious negative peace, where the Negro passively accepted his unjust plight, to a substance-filled positive peace, where all men will respect the dignity and worth of human personality. Actually, we who engage in nonviolent direct action are not the creators of tension. We merely bring to the surface the hidden tension that is already alive. We bring it out in the open where it can be seen and dealt with. Like a boil that can never be cured as long as it is covered up but must be opened with all its pus-flowing ugliness to the natural medicines of air and light, injustice must likewise be exposed, with all of the tension its exposing creates, to the light of human conscience and the air of national opinion before it can be cured.

In your statement you asserted that our actions, even though peaceful, must be condemned because they precipitate violence. But can this assertion be logically made? Isn't this like condemning the robbed man because his possession of money precipitated the evil act of robbery? Isn't this like condemning Socrates because his unswerving commitment to truth and his philosophical delvings precipitated the misguided popular mind to make him drink the hemlock? Isn't this like condemning Jesus because His unique God-Consciousness and never-ceasing devotion to His will precipitated the evil act of crucifixion? We must come to see, as federal courts have consistently affirmed, that it is immoral to urge an individual to withdraw his efforts to gain his basic constitutional rights because the quest precipitates violence. Society must protect the robbed and punish the robber.

I had also hoped that the white moderate would reject the myth of time. I received a letter this morning from a white brother in

Texas which said: "All Christians know that the colored people will receive equal rights eventually, but it is possible that you are in too great of a religious hurry. It has taken Christianity almost two thousand years to accomplish what it has. The teachings of Christ take time to come to earth." All that is said here grows out of a tragic misconception of time. It is the strangely irrational notion that there is something in the very flow of time that will inevitably cure all ills. Actually time is neutral. It can be used either destructively or constructively. I am coming to feel that the people of ill-will have used time much more effectively than the people of good will. We will have to repent in this generation not merely for the vitriolic words and actions of the bad people, but for the appalling silence of good people. We must come to see that human progress never rolls in on wheels of inevitability. It comes through the tireless efforts and persistent work of men willing to be coworkers with God, and without this hard work time itself becomes an ally of the forces of social stagnation. We must use time creatively, and forever realize that the time is always ripe to do right. Now is the time to make real the promise of democracy, and transform our pending national elegy into a creative psalm of brotherhood. Now is the time to lift our national policy from the quicksand of racial injustice to the solid rock of human dignity.

I stand in the middle of two opposing forces in the Negro community. One is a force of complacency made up of Negroes who, as a result of long years of oppression, have been so completely drained of self-respect and a sense of "somebodiness" that they have adjusted to segregation, and of a few Negroes in the middle class who, because of a degree of academic and economic security, and because at points they profit by segregation, have unconsciously become insensitive to the problems of the masses. The other force is one of bitterness and hatred, and comes perilously close to advocating violence. It is expressed in the various black-nationalist groups that are springing up over the nation, the largest and best known being Elijah Muhammad's Muslim movement. This movement is nourished by the contemporary frustration over the continued existence of racial discrimination. It is made up of people who have lost faith in America, who have absolutely repudiated Christianity, and who have concluded that the white man is an incurable "devil." I have tried to stand between these two forces, saying that we need not follow the "do-nothingism" of the complacent or the hatred and despair of the black nationalists. There is the more excellent way of love and nonviolent protest. I'm grateful to God that, through the Negro church, the dimension of nonviolence entered our struggle. If this philosophy had not emerged, I am convinced that by now many streets of the South would be flowing with floods of blood. And I am further convinced that if our white brothers dismiss as "rabble-rousers" and "outside agitators" those of us who are working through the channels of nonviolent direct action and refuse to support our nonviolent efforts, millions of Negroes, out of frustration and despair, will seek solace and security in black nationalist ideologies, a development that will lead inevitably to a frightening racial nightmare.

Oppressed people cannot remain oppressed forever. The urge for freedom will eventually come. This is what happened to the American Negro. Something within has reminded him of his birthright of freedom; something without has reminded him that he can gain it. Consciously, and unconsciously, he has been swept in by what the Germans call the Zeitgeist, and with his black brothers of Africa, and his brown and yellow brothers of Asia, South America, and the Caribbean, he is moving with a sense of cosmic urgency toward the promised land of racial justice. Recognizing this vital urge that has engulfed the Negro community, one should readily understand public demonstrations. The Negro has many pent-up resentments and latent frustrations. He has to get them out. So let him march sometime; let him have his prayer pilgrimages to the city hall; understand why he must have sit-ins and freedom rides. If his repressed emotions do not come out in these nonviolent ways, they will come out in ominous expressions of violence. This is not a threat; it is a fact of history. So I have not said to my people "get rid of your discontent." But I have tried to say that this normal and healthy discontent can be channelized through the creative outlet of nonviolent direct action. Now this approach is being dismissed as extremist. I must admit that I was initially disappointed in being so categorized.

But as I continued to think about the matter I gradually gained a bit of satisfaction from being considered an extremist. Was not Jesus an extremist in love? "Love your enemies, bless them that curse you, pray for them that despitefully use you." Was not Amos an extremist for justice? "Let justice roll down like water and righteousness like a mighty stream." Was not Paul an extremist for the gospel of Jesus Christ? "I bear in my body the marks of the Lord Jesus." Was not Martin Luther an extremist? "Here I stand; I can do none other so help me God." Was not John Bunyan an extremist? "I will stay in jail to the end of my days before I make a butchery of my conscience." Was not Abraham Lincoln an extremist? "This nation cannot survive half slave and half free." Was not Thomas Jefferson an extremist? "We hold these truths to be self-evident, that all men are created equal." So the question is not whether we will be extremist but what kind of extremist will we be. Will we be extremists for hate—or will we be extremists for love? Will we be extremists for the preservation of injustice—or will we be extremists for the cause of justice? In that dramatic scene on Calvary's hill, three men were crucified. We must not forget that all three were crucified for the same crime—the crime of extremism. Two were extremists for immorality, and thusly fell below their environment. The other, Jesus Christ, was an extremist for love, truth, and goodness, and thereby rose above his environment. So, after all, maybe the South, the nation, and the world are in dire need of creative extremists.

I hope the church as a whole will meet the challenge of this decisive hour. But even if the church does not come to the aid of justice, I have no despair about the future. I have no fear about the outcome of our struggle in Birmingham, even if our motives are frequently misunderstood. We will reach the goal of freedom in Birmingham and all over the nation, because the goal of America is freedom. Abused and scorned though we may be, our destiny is tied up with the destiny of America. Before the pilgrims landed at Plymouth we were here. Before the pen of Jefferson etched across the pages of history the majestic words of the Declaration of Independence, we were here. For more than two centuries our fore-parents labored in this country without wages; they made cotton king, and they built the homes of their masters in the midst of brutal injustice and shameful humiliation—and yet out of a bottomless vitality they continued to thrive and develop. If the inexpressible cruelties of slavery could not stop us, the opposition we now face will surely fail. We will win our freedom because the sacred heritage of our nation and the eternal will of God are embodied in our echoing demands.

# GEORGE GRANT TO JUDGE ROY MOORE:

*American writer, 1954–*

President Theodore Roosevelt said it clearly and distinctly: "The nation should be ruled by the Ten Commandments." This was not mere caprice or prejudice on the great man's part. Instead, it was a clear comprehension of the foundations of freedom.

The fact is, apart from the succinct standard of the Ten Commandments, liberty is left to the whims of fashion and fancy, it is left to the benevolence of the elite and the beneficence of the powerful.

Fisher Ames, one of our most erudite Founding Fathers said it well: "Every considerate friend of civil liberty, in order to be consistent with himself must be the friend of the Bible. Indeed, no man can be a sound lawyer in this land who is not well read in the ethics of Moses and the virtues of Jesus."

The fact is, without the unchanging standard, the unwavering foundation of ethics outlined in the Ten Commandments, we are left to the mercy of momentary affectations of juridical discretion. Any student of history can quickly testify, there is little protection for freedom in that. There is little surety for justice in that. There is little solace for the poor in that.

The Ten Commandments afford us the cornerstone against which our Bill of Rights is secured. Without them, those precious constitutional guarantees are jeopardized by the fickle fortunes of politics. The Ten Commandments afford us the buttress against which our legal system is moored. Without them our treasured judicial precedents are left to drift in a sea of uncertain tides and roiling storms. Indeed, without them we are all relegated to a rambunctious relativism.

But perhaps the worst effect of dispensing with the immutable certainty of the Ten Commandments is the proliferation of legislation and litigation that would inevitably result. When sure and secure standards—long tested by time and confirmed by experience—when such standards are dropped in favor of the passing poses of man's presumed ingenuity, a flood of heedless, needless governmental regulations and clarifications is sure to follow.

As G.K. Chesterton has wisely observed, "If men will not be governed by the Ten Commandments, they shall be governed by the ten thousand commandments." When the big laws are abandoned, you don't get anarchism; you don't get libertarianism; you get governmentalism. You don't get fewer restrictions on personal freedom, fewer restraints on personal behavior, fewer intrusions on personal intimacy; you get more. Lots more.

A nation that rejects the decrees of God inevitably becomes subject to the decrees of the demigod. A nation that shuts its eyes to the dumb certainties of experience and flies in the face of all reason will most assuredly face a sterner judgment—the judgment of fellow citizens gone mad with power and privilege. Sow the wind; reap the whirlwind.

The whimpering, simpering ACLU, the gossip-mongering liberal media, the professional complainers that seem to infest the corridors of power in Washington these days, and all the other foes of our own household have a bold plan for America—a plan to take us all far down the road to ruin. Thankfully men like you stand foursquare across that path. I want to pledge our commitment to join you there. May we never waver—for the sake of freedom. May we never falter—in the cause of liberty. May we never abandon—this nation, under God.

God gave us the Ten Commandments to save us from the ten thousand commandments—and every other malignancy conceived by the mind of sinful man. May we have the wisdom to appropriate the grace He has thus shed upon us all.

*Gardens*

*Gardening is a means of grace. There is just something about a garden that restores a sense of balance and serenity to a life harried by the tyranny of the urgent. Anne Scott James is a contemporary English literary critic. Her words of counsel to her daughter afford the amateur gardener a glimpse of the significance of the most ordinary of pleasures. Likewise, the other selections here portray the sense of the holy that may be derived from the wholly worldly.*

# ANNE SCOTT-JAMES TO HER DAUGHTER CLARE:
### ❧ *British critic and journalist, 1913–* ☙

I have written much this year about the beautiful and the good.
Enthusiastic gardening writers are apt to get carried away by the
many lovely things they see and it is easy for the reader to get the
impression that all English gardens are beautiful, luxuriant, fragrant,
mysterious, rich in surprises, painted with an artist's palette, miracles
of harmonious planting, and so on and so forth. The eye is carried
admiringly upwards, downwards, sideways etc. until one is almost
squinting with delight. But there are bad gardens, too, which merci-
fully one soon forgets, like the pains of childbirth, but perhaps as the
year ends one should be a little more critical and ask an unusual
question. What makes a bad garden?

One common cause of bad gardening afflicts the keen gardener,
not the lazy one. He (or she) has fallen under too many influences.
He reads a lot, sees a lot, and takes advice from everybody, so that
his garden is full of conflicting ideas. A sensitive gardener with
catholic tastes may grow many things from lime-loving alpines to
peat-loving pieris, but he will keep them apart, providing a different
background for each. But I know gardens where you can see, all in

one eyeful, specimen Japanese maples in the lawn, a cottage border with hollyhocks and pansies to one side, and a knot garden somewhere in the middle. The result is not the expression of one gardener's taste, but a mess of pottage. Often the gardener himself is not happy with the result and makes bad worse by consulting more and more people, who each give different advice.

Bad gardens of another sort are created by the unbridled use of colour, and summer bedding plants are the chief culprits. The clash of the harsh colours of marigolds, busy lizzies, Salvia splendens and begonias gives a shock rather than a happy glow. The gardener is often technically skilled and raises perfect plants in the greenhouse, but he gives no thought to their arrangement. You may well say that no garden is a bad garden if the gardener likes it, and you are right. But it is gardening at a low level. No outsider having seen the garden once would want to look at it twice, for it can be comprehended at a glance, and there is nothing to see in winter.

Another class of bad garden is the product of too much money. It is packed with showy and expensive garden furnishings which dominate the plants. White seats and white pyramids for supporting roses give the look of a hotel ballroom, and even worse are those costly swings upholstered in cretonne patterned with tropical flowers which are larger and brighter than anything which grows. Miss

Jekyll thought that garden furniture should be an inconspicuous comfort, and that seats should be in dark colours, preferably brown, and I cannot forgive the restorers of Monet's famous garden at Giverny for painting the seats and bridge in the brightest green in the paint manufacturer's showcard. A swimming-pool can also be an eyesore. If a gardener wants an athlete's pool with diving boards, changing rooms and a shower, why doesn't he hide it away in a hedged enclosure?

Run-of-the-mill gardeners like you and me will have bad patches in our gardens, perhaps ill-planned steps or paths or planting mistakes, but I hope there is none of the real ugliness which arises from pretentiousness or from lifting ideas indiscriminately instead of making a personal choice.

ANNE SCOTT-JAMES TO HER DAUGHTER CLARE:
*British critic and journalist, 1913–*

One for facts, one for ideas, one for amusement, one for ecstasy. I have been pondering on which four books I would choose for a learner-gardener's bookshelf, assuming that the beginner, though ignorant of gardening, would be otherwise literate.

As a reference book of facts, the Reader's Digest *Encyclopaedia of Garden Plants and Flowers* was formerly unique, and mine is falling apart from use. But now there is a newer blockbuster, the R. H. S. Gardener's *Encyclopaedia of Plants and Flowers*, edited by the incomparable Chris Brickell. This lists 8,000 plants, classified according to their function in the garden, shrubs, climbers, perennials, rock plants, and so on, with colour photographs, descriptions and growing instructions, and breaks new ground by marking every plant for hardiness with one, two or three stars. The Reader's Digest volume has fewer plants (3,000), but is easier for quick reference, the plants being listed in ABC order. To have one or the other is essential.

There are many contestants for the book of ideas. Graham Stuart Thomas's *Perennial Garden Plants* ranks very high, for it is not only a dictionary of the best perennials, but is strong on the difficult subject of plant associations (what to plant with what), of which Graham Thomas is a master. Of the golden oldies, V. Sackville-West's *Garden Book* is inspirational, and the modesty with which she writes is heartwarming when you consider how deep was her knowledge and how grand her background; she never patronised, but distilled her experience thoughtfully for the humbler gardener. But my final choice would go to *The Well-Tempered Garden* by Christopher Lloyd, for though the themes are serious, the tone is human and witty.

For amusement, I would choose every time, *Elizabeth and Her German Garden*, by Elizabeth von Arnim, and usually it is out of my bookshelf and beside my bed. Elizabeth was a clever, attractive, waspish young creature who married a bad-tempered German count in 1889 and made a garden on his estate in Prussia. She is cruelly witty about her neighbors, her staff, and particularly her husband, whom she refers to as the Man of Wrath, but she had a genuine passion for nature and for her wildish garden full of lilacs and roses, poppies and columbines, lavender and pinks, in an isolated countryside of pine forests and cornfields. Though her words are sharp, they have a poetic beauty, so that the book is both a comedy and an idyll.

It could almost count as a book of ecstasy, but I think it would be nice to have one book which would take the reader right out of the garden and into the wild. *On the Eaves of the World*, by Reginald

Farrer, does just that. Farrer was a plant-hunter, and when World War One broke out he was exploring in a part of China so remote that it was many months before he heard the news. In beautiful prose, he describes the joys of looking for plants in the wild, making light of the dangers and hardships. When he spots the glorious Moutan Peony in a copse in the mountains he plunges into the scrub as excited as a schoolboy, and when he reaches the peony—that enormous single blossom of pure white, with featherlings of deepest maroon radiating from the base of the petals—he remains for a long time quietly worshipping it, before returning 'at last in the dusk in high contentment.'

When looking at the many exotic flowers which are now quite at home in English gardens, it adds to one's appreciation to recall that the botanists who discovered them were as intrepid as Christopher Columbus or Dr. Livingstone.

# GEORGE GRANT TO HIS WIFE KAREN:
*American writer, 1954–*

Adjacent to Lambeth Palace just across the Thames from Westminster is one of London's most delightful gardens. There, within the tiny churchyard of the St. Mary Parish, is a carefully tended walled plot bursting with color and fragrance. A narrow brick-lined pathway winds through lush beds of forget-me-nots, polyanthus, and crown imperial fritillaries. What appear to be haphazard clumps of lilac, viburnum, and philadelphus are linked integrally to one another by a wide wavy border planted with alchemilla, nepeta, and several other sturdy herbaceous plants that I've never quite been able to identify. There are assorted blooming primroses, lillies, and canterbury bells in spring and snap-dragons, hardy geraniums, and lavender in summer. Along one wall, in front of a magnificent wisteria, is a bed redolent with herbs—basil, thyme, oregano, and cilantro. There is parsley among the hollyhocks, honeysuckle twisted round the roses, and tiger lilies peaking through the shrubby euphorbias. It is a hard-won taste of paradise planted in the midst of a hustle-bustle urban sprawl.

Though the celebrated English gardens of Hever Castle, of Sissinghurst, or of Glyndebourne are certainly more spectacular, it is this little parish vicar's garden that epitomizes for me all that a garden ought to be. Its personal scale, its wide-ranging palette, and its orderly conception portray a distinctly practical vision of both the possibilities and the limitations of this poor fallen world.

As if to underscore this truth, a little bronze plaque adorning one corner of the garden declares: "A good theology will invariably produce a good garden." The first time I read that I chuckled and quickly dismissed it as just another bit of gardener's hyperbole. But then, the more I thought about it the more I began realize that the plaque's epigram actually conveys a uniquely Scriptural worldview.

A good theology is more than the sum of its parts. While it is composed of certain essential dogmas and doctrines, each of those essentials must also be carefully related to all the others. It sees all too clearly the crucial connection between the profound and the mundane. While it wisely attends to the minutest of details, it also remains fully cognizant of how those details affect the bigger picture. It places as much significance on the bits and pieces as it does on the totals.

A good theology is good for the soul. But it is also good for the world. Its spiritual vision gives vitality to all that it touches—from flower gardens and herbiaries to nation states and cultures—simply because the integrity of that vision ultimately depends as much on a balanced Biblical worldview as on a solid Scriptural soteriology. Its attention to heavenly concerns is integrally bound to its fulfillment of earthly responsibilities.

Of course, actually making that connection between heavenly concerns and earthly responsibilities is never easy. We are all constantly tugged between piety and practicality, between devotion and duty, between communion with God and calling in the world. Like tending a well-groomed garden, honing a balanced Biblical worldview involves both the drudgery of daily labor and the high ideals of faith, hope, and love. But the results are always worth the extra effort.

A good theology—with its comprehensive worldview—inevitably affects the world for good. While a bad theology—with its fragmented worldview—sows only tares.

# Grief

*It is not likely that any words are sufficient in times of grief—
even when they come from the pens of the wisest of the wise.
There is no amount of philosophizing, no measure of determination, and no course of preparation that can sufficiently establish a heart against storms of sorrow during times of loss.
Nevertheless, it is of the essence of our nature to try. And who
better to try than the incomparable Samuel Johnson, the
esteemed Edward Payson, and the versatile John Watson.
Johnson was of course the great eighteenth-century English wit
and man of letters. Payson was a popular nineteenth-century
American Puritan pastor from New York, and Watson was the
famed author of the nineteenth century classic,* Beyond the
Bonnie Briar Bush. *Each crafts words of compassion
with the touch of a master.*

# Samuel Johnson to Dr. Lawrence upon the loss of Lawrence's wife:

*⊶ English writer and lexicographer, 1709–1784 ⊷*

At a time when all your friends ought to shew their kindness, and with a character which ought to make all that know you your friends, you may wonder that you have yet heard nothing from me.

The loss, dear Sir, which you have lately suffered, I felt many years ago, and know therefore how much has been taken from you, and how little help can be had from consolation. He that outlives a wife whom he has long loved, sees himself disjoined from the only mind that has the same hopes, and fears, and interest; from the only companion with whom he has shared much good or evil; and with whom he could set his mind at liberty to retrace the past or antici-pate the future. The continuity of being is lacerated; the settled course of sentiment and action is stopped; and life stands suspended and motionless, till it is driven by external causes into a new channel. But the time of suspense is dreadful.

Our first recourse in this distressed solitude, is, perhaps for want of habitual piety, to a gloomy acquiescence in necessity. Of two mor-tal beings, one must lose the other; but surely there is a higher and

better comfort to be drawn from the consideration of that
Providence which watches over all, and a belief that the living and
the dead are equally in the hands of God, who will reunite those
whom he has separated; or who sees that it is best not to reunite. I
am, dear Sir, your most affectionate, and most humble servant.

---

### Rev. Edward Payson to his parents upon the loss of his sister, their daughter, Grata:
*American pastor, 1783–1827*

You will probably hear from poor brother Rand before you receive
this letter, that you have one child less on earth to comfort you in
the decline of life; that dear, dear Grata has gone before you to
heaven. I cannot hope to console you; but I do hope that your sur-
viving children will feel bound to do every thing in their power to
make up your loss, by increased filial affection and concern for your
happiness. I cannot mourn for Grata. How much suffering of body
and mind has she escaped by her early departure! But I mourn for
poor brother Rand, for his motherless children, and for you. It
would be some consolation to you, could you know how much she
was beloved, how greatly her loss is lamented, how much good she

did, and how loudly she is praised by all who knew her. I doubt not that hundreds mourn for her, and feel her loss almost or quite as much as do her relatives. Mr. H., who preached her funeral sermon, gave her a most exalted character.

Many, many prayers have been offered up, both here and at Gorham, that you may be supported and comforted when the tidings reach you; and I hope and trust they will be answered. Thanks be to God that you are loved and blessed by many who never saw you, on account of your children. Mr. Rand feels great hopes that her loss will be blessed to his church and people; and that she will do more good in her death, than she has done in her life; and from what I saw at the funeral, I cannot but indulge similar hopes. The suddenness of her departure makes the other world appear very near; and she seems as much, and even more alive, than she did before. I preached with reference to the subject yesterday; and could not but hope that her death might be blessed to some of my people, or at least to some of the church.

### REV. JOHN WATSON TO A FRIEND ON THE ANNIVERSARY OF HER LITTLE CHILD'S DEATH:

*Scottish author and pastor, 1838–1907*

My dear friend, have you read The Blessed Damozel? "They are safe who are with Jesus where they follow the Lamb to Living Fountains of Water." And the day has now broken.

But I am writing in the train to send you a quotation from that Scots saint Archbishop Leighton. In a letter of his to his sister on the loss of her little boy: "Sweet thing, and is he so quickly laid to sleep? Happy he. Though we shall have no more the pleasure of his lisping and laughing, he shall have no more of the pain of crying or of dying, or of being sick: And hath wholly escaped the trouble of schooling, and all other sufferings of boys, and the riper and deeper griefs of riper years. This poor life being all along nothing but many sorrows and many deaths. John is but gone an hour or two sooner to bed, and we are undressing to follow. The more we put off the love of this present world and all things superfluous beforehand, we shall have the less to do when we lie down.

# Justice

*A* true sense of justice does not come naturally to most of us. All too often we must be jolted by the horrors of prejudice, discrimination, or caprice before we are willing to step outside our comfort zone and stand for the despised, the rejected, or the victimized. L.B. Webster was jolted, as he relates in his letter to his wife, when he was required to participate in the U.S. Army's forced dispossession of the Cherokee people early in the nineteenth century. Former president Theodore Roosevelt and former Confederate general and slave-trader Nathan Bedford Forrest both had their sense of justice awakened by the horrors of war. In each case, the tenants of equity were engrafted upon their consciences, as their letters so obviously demonstrate.

# LIEUTENANT L.B. WEBSTER WITH THE CHEROKEE ALONG THE "TRAIL OF TEARS," TO HIS WIFE:

*American military officer, 1784–1842*

I do not intend to say more than two or three words to you in this, I feel so very bad at having missed a letter from you, which was sent from her to Fort Butler the day before I arrived here, and I do not expect to get it for two or three days to come. In the mean time I shall feel very cross & must grumble a little; but I will not scold my sweet wife, so do not be frightened.

I left Fort Butler on the 19th in charge of 800 Cherokees. I had not an officer along to assist me, and only my own company as a guard. Of course I have as much to do as I could attend to. But I experienced no difficulty in getting them along, other than what arose from fatigue, and this toughness of the roads over the mountains; which are the worst I ever saw. I arrived with about one hundred more than what I started with. Many having joined me on the march. We were eight days in making the journey and it was pitiful to behold the women and children, who suffered exceedingly, as they were all obliged to walk, with the exception of the sick. I am to remain here and await the arrival of the remainder of the regiment, which is expected in about two weeks. After which (and I have it from very good authority, Gen. Scott himself), two or three regiments of artillery will be ordered onto the northern frontier, about Plattsburgh and Sackettshaboun, and there is no doubt but our regiment will be one of them.

How would you like to go on to Brownsville and Geneva my dear girl? I know you would like it; and I am in hopes that six weeks will find you on the way. As soon as Gen. Eustis arrives here I shall apply for a leave of absence and if I should be so fortunate as to obtain it, it will not take me long to fly to you; and we will then soon be on our way to the north. But should I be obliged to march with the Troops, and they will probably go through Ken. And up the Ohio to the Lakes, I hope you will find some means of joining me, say at Brownsville, or is this asking too much from your soldiers life? I am sure you will be a widow if I do not see you in two or three months— I can't stand it much longer, though I am now in excellent health. It appears to me that I have hardly been with you a week since we were married. Is it not abominable? Christopher is here, and I am now writing in his tent. He desires particularly to be remembered to you, as also Major Whitney. Capt. Vinton is at Ross Landing.

I suppose you have heard that the emigration of the Cherokees is suspended till September, and that they are to remain in depot about here till that time. They have all been collected with the exception of those to be brought down by Gen. Eustis. We have seven or eight thousand encamped about us, and they are the most quiet people you ever saw.

I omitted to mention that I have three regular ministers of the gospel in my party, and that we have preaching or prayer meetings every night while on the march. And you may well imagine that under the peculiar circumstances of the case, among those sublime mountains and in the dark forests with the thunder often sounding in the distance that nothing could be worse. I always looked on with a cry ascending to Heaven, calling out to Him who alone can and will grant grace to fall upon my guilty head despite my being one of the instruments of oppression.

My love to your father and mother and little kats. And remembrance to all friends. I have only received one of your letters, but shall write you again when I get halve of another. I have written now more than I intended.

Do my dear wife take care of yourself, and I know Heaven will protect you. You must forgive your very bad Husband for deserting you so long. I feel guilty on account of it. God bless my dear good wife.

# THEODORE ROOSEVELT TO THE SOLDIERS OF THE GREAT WAR:

*American author, adventurer, and president, 1858–1919*

The whole teaching of the New Testament is actually foreshadowed in Micah's verse. Do justice; and therefore fight valiantly against those that stand for the reign of Moloch and Beelzebub on this earth.

Love mercy; treat your enemies well; succor the afflicted; treat every woman as if she were your sister; care for the little children; and be tender with the old and helpless.

Walk humbly; you will do so if you study the life and teachings of the Savior, walking in His steps. Remember: the most perfect machinery of government will not keep us as a nation from destruction if there is not within us a soul. No abounding of material prosperity shall avail us if our spiritual senses atrophy.

The foes of our own household will surely prevail against us unless there be in our people an inner life which finds its outward expression in a morality like unto that preached by the seers and prophets of God when the grandeur that was Greece and the glory that was Rome still lay in the future.

The most dangerous form of sentimental debauch is to give expression to good wishes on behalf of virtue while you do nothing about it. Justice is not merely words. It is to be translated into acts.

---

## NATHAN BEDFORD FORREST TO THE FORMER SLAVES OF MEMPHIS:
*American Confederate general, 1821–1877*

We were born on the same soil, breathe the same air, live on the same land, and so why should we not be brothers and sisters?

---

## THE PROPHET MICAH TO THE PEOPLE OF ANCIENT JERUSALEM AND JUDAH:
*Prophet in Israel, eighth century B.C.*

He has shown you, O man, what is good and what the Lord requires of you: but to do justice, and to love mercy, and to walk humbly with your God.

# Leadership

*W*hat is it exactly that makes a great leader? What constitutes genuine leadership? What character traits are necessary to
steer men and nations into the way they should go? How may
we train young people to become such leaders as they ought to
be—and as we need them to be? How are we to "study well"
that which is both "the most tangible and intangible" simulta-
neously? These are particularly relevant questions in this difficult day of profound leaderlessness. There can be little doubt
that we are the most over-managed yet under-led generation in
recent memory—thus, our great imperious task is to somehow
buck the trend and wrestle with such questions. Who better to
help us do so than America's singular founding father George
Washington, England's Lord Protector Oliver Cromwell, and
the great Southern military tactician Stonewall Jackson?

# GEORGE WASHINGTON AT VALLEY FORGE TO HIS CRITICS IN THE CONTINENTAL CONGRESS:

*❊ American patriot, planter, and president, 1732–1799 ❊*

Though I have been tender heretofore of giving any opinion, or lodging complaints, as the change in that department took place contrary to my judgment, and the consequences thereof were predicted; yet, finding that the inactivity of the army, whether for want of provisions, clothes, or other essentials, as charged to my account, not only by the common vulgar but by those in power, it is time to speak plain in exculpation of myself. With truth, then, I can declare that no man in my opinion ever had his measures more impeded than I have, by every department of the army.

As a proof of the little benefit received from a clothier-general, and as a further proof of the inability of an army, under the circumstances of this, to perform the common duties of soldiers…we have, by a field-return this day made, no less than two thousand eight hundred and ninety-eight men now in camp unfit for duty, because they are barefoot and otherwise naked. Since the 4th instant, our numbers fit for duty, from the hardships and exposures they have undergone, particularly on account of blankets (numbers having been obliged, and still are, to sit up all night by fires, instead of taking comfortable rest in a natural and common way), have decreased near two thousand men.

We find gentlemen, without knowing whether the army was really going into winter-quarters or not reprobating the measure as much as if they thought the soldiers were made of stocks or stones, and equally insensible of frost and snow.

But what makes this matter still more extraordinary in my eye is, that these very gentlemen, who were well apprized of the nakedness of the troops from ocular demonstration ... should think a winter's campaign, and the covering of these States (New Jersey and Pennsylvania) from the invasion of an enemy, so easy and practicable a business. I can assure those gentlemen, that it is a much easier and less distressing thing to draw remonstrances in a comfortable room by a good fireside, than to occupy a cold, bleak hill, and sleep under frost and snow, without clothes or blankets. However, although they seem to have little feeling for the naked and distressed soldiers, I feel superabundantly for them, and, from my soul, I pity those miseries, which it is neither in my power to relieve or prevent.

It is for these reasons, therefore, that I have dwelt upon the subject; and it adds not a little to my other difficulties and distress to find, that much more is expected of me than is possible to be performed, and that upon the ground of safety and policy I am obliged to conceal the true state of the army from public view, and thereby expose myself to detraction and calumny.

---

### STONEWALL JACKSON TO A JUNIOR ARMY OFFICER:
*American Confederate general, 1824–1863*

What is life without honor? Degradation is worse than death. True leadership comprehends this full well.

# OLIVER CROMWELL TO HIS SON HENRY:
### *Lord Protector of England, 1599–1658*

I have seen your Letter writ unto Mr. Secretary Thurloe; and do find thereby that you are very apprehensive of the carriage of some persons with you, towards yourself and the public affairs.

I do believe there may be some particular persons who are not very well pleased with the present condition of things, and may be apt to show their discontent of things, and may be apt to show their discontent as they have opportunity; but this should not make too great impressions in you. Time and patience may work them to a better frame of spirit, and bring them to see that which, for the present, seems to be hid from them; especially if they shall see your moderation and love towards them, if they are found in other ways towards you. Which I earnestly desire you to study and endeavor, al [*sic.*] that lies in you. Whereof both you and I too shall have the comfort, whatsoever the issue and event thereof be.

*Why are we here? What is the meaning of it all? At one time or another we all have to face these universal questions. Indeed, to find any semblance of balance, perspective, and purposefulness in our short sojourn on earth, we must honestly and substantively wrestle with such metaphysical issues. There is no avoiding it—regardless of how hard we may try. We may be imminently practical in our approach to them, as was the department store mogul Marshall Field; or floridly lyrical as was the Scottish poet laureate Robert Burns; or dynamically philosophical as was the Danish theologian Soren Kierkegaard. But one way or another we too must confront the matter.*

### SAMUEL JOHNSON TO JAMES BOSWELL:
*English writer and lexicographer, 1709–1784*

Reflect that life, like every other blessing, derives its value from its use alone.

---

### SOREN KIERKEGAARD TO HARLAN HALVERSON:
*Danish religious philosopher, 1813–1855*

Life can only be understood backwards, but it must be lived forwards.

---

### JOHN KEATS TO ELIZABETH JOHNSON:
*English poet, 1795–1821*

Let us not go hurrying about collecting honey, bee-like buzzing here and there for a knowledge of what is not to be arrived at, but let us open our leaves like a flower, and be receptive, budding patiently under the hand of providence.

# Robert Burns to a Young Friend:

*Scottish poet, 1759–1796*

I land ha'e thought, my youthfu' friend,
A something to have sent you,
Though it should serve nae other end
Than just a kind memento;
But how the subject theme may gang,
Let time and chance determine;
Perhaps it may turn out a sang,
Perhaps turn out a sermon.

Ye'll try the world soon, my lad
And, Andrew dear, believe me,
Ye'll find mankind an unco squad,
And muckle they might grieve ye:
For care and trouble set your thought,
E'en when your end's attained;
And a' your views may come to nought,
Where every nerve is strained.

I'll no say men are villains a';
The real, hardened wicked,
Wha ha'e nae check but human law,
Are to a few restricted:
But och, mankind are unco weak,
An' little to be trusted;
If self the wavering balance shake,
It's rarely right adjusted!

Yet they wha fa' in fortune's strife,
Their fate we should na censure,
For still th' important end of life
They equally may answer;
A man may ha'e an honest heart,
Though poortith hourly stare him;
A man may tak' a neebor's part,
Yet nae ha'e cash to spare him.

Aye free, aff han your story tell,
When wi' a bosom crony;
But still keep something to yoursel'
Ye scarcely tell to ony.

Conceal yoursel' as weel's ye can
Fra critical dissection;
But keek through every other man,
Wi' sharpened, sly inspection.

The sacred lowe o' weel-placed love,
Luxuriantly indulge it;
But never tempt th' illicit rove,
Though naething should divulge it.
I wave the quantum o' the sin,
The hazard of concealing:
But och! It hardens a' within,
And petrified the feeling!

To catch dame Fortune's golden smile,
Assiduous wait upon her;
And gather gear by every wile
That's justified by honour;
Not for to hide it in a hedge,
Nor for a train attendant;
But for the glorious privilege
Of being independent.

The fear o' hell's a hangman's whip
To haud the wretch in order;
But where ye feel your honour grip,
Let that aye be your border;
Its slightest touches, instant pause—
Debar a' side pretences;
And resolutely keep its laws,
Uncaring consequences.

The Great Creator to revere,
Must sure become the creature;
But still the preaching cant forbear,
And e'en the rigid feature:
Yet ne'er with wits profane to range,
Be complaisance extended;
An atheist's laugh's a poor exchange
For Deity offended!

When ranting round in pleasure's ring,
Religion may be blinded;
Or if she gi'e a random sting,
It may be little minded;

But when on life we're tempest-driven,
A conscience but a canker
A correspondence fixed wi' Heaven
Is sure a noble anchor!

Adieu, dear amiable youth!
Your heart can ne'er be wanting;
May Prudence, Fortitude, and Truth,
Erect your brow undaunting!
In ploughman phrase, "God send you speed,"
Still daily to grow wiser!
And may you better reck the rede [advice],
Than ever did th' adviser!

---

# THE APOSTLE PAUL TO THE CHRISTIANS IN THE CITY OF ROME:

*Christian apostle and missionary, c. 10–65*

Let love be genuine; hate what is evil; hold fast to what is good; love one another with brotherly affection; outdo one another in showing honor. Never flag in zeal; be aglow with the Spirit; serve the Lord. Rejoice in your hope; be patient in tribulation; be constant in prayer.

## Mark Twain to his daughter:
❧ *American author and humorist, 1835–1910* ❧

Let us endeavor to live so that when we come to die, even the undertaker will be sorry.

———————

## Marshall Field to his son:
❧ *American merchant, 1834–1906* ❧

There are twelve things I wish you to remember: 1. The value of time. 2. The success of perseverence. 3. The pleasure of working. 4. The dignity of simplicity. 5. The worth of character. 6. The power of kindness. 7. The influence of example. 8. The obligation of duty. 10. The virtue of patience. 11. The improvement of talent. 12. The joy of origination.

———————

## William Hazlitt to Charles Mackenzie:
❧ *British essayist, 1778–1830* ❧

The art of life is to know how to enjoy a little and to endure much.

# Love

*Has there ever been a subject that has elicited more advice than the subject of love? And is there any wonder why? Matters of the heart have occupied talent and ingenuity of every human discipline and occupation. Here soldiers and statesmen wax as eloquent as poets and musicians. Here the muse enlivens even the coarsest and crustiest of souls. Here we have fine mentors in the gentle arts in the Elizabethan lyricist Edmund Spencer, the Scots chronicler Robert Burns, the Victorian novelist Jane Austen, the French scientist Pierre Curie, the Jewish king Solomon, the British adventurer Walter Raleigh, and several others. Each captures a different facet of this obstinately marvelous thing called love.*

### Edmund Spenser to Benjamin Callow:
*English poet, c. 1552–1599*

Gather the rose of love whilst yet is time.

---

### Robert Burns to John Richmond:
*Scottish poet, 1759–1796*

And let us mind, faint heart ne'er won
A lady fair.
Wha does the utmost, that he can
Will shyles do mair.

---

### George Herbert to Frances Croyle:
*English poet, 1593–1633*

Scorn no man's love though of a mean degree: love is a present for a
mighty king; much less make any one thine enemy.

# VINCENT VAN GOGH TO HIS BROTHER THEO:

*Dutch painter, 1853–1890*

Love many things, for therein lies true strength, and whosoever loves much performs much, and can accomplish much, and what is done in love is oft done well.

---

# THOMAS D'URFEY TO HIS NEPHEW:

*English barrister, 1781–1855*

Take not the first refusal ill though now she won't, anon she will.

# Jane Austen to her niece Fanny Knight:
### ◦{ *British writer, 1775–1817* }◦

I feel the sterling worth of such a young Man and the desirableness of your growing in love with him again. I recommend this most thoroughly. There are such beings in the World perhaps, one in a Thousand, as the Creature You and I should think perfection, Where Grace and Spirit are united to Worth, where the Manners are equal to the Heart and Understanding, but such a person may not come in your way, or if he does, he may not be the eldest son of a Man of Fortune, the Brother of your particular friend, and belonging to your own County.

Think of all this Fanny. Mr. J. P. has advantages which do not often meet in one person. His only fault indeed seems Modesty. If he were less modest, he would be more agreable, speak louder and look Impudenter—and is not it a fine Character of which Modesty is the only defect? I have no doubt that he will get more lively and more like yourselves as he is more with you—he will catch your ways if he belongs to you. And as to there being any objection from his Goodness, from the danger of his becoming even Evangelical, I cannot admit that. I am by no means convinced that we ought not all to be Evangelicals, and am at least persuaded that they who are so from Reason and Feeling, must be happiest and safest.

Do not be frightened from the connection by your Brothers having most wit. Wisdom is better than Wit, and in the long run will certainly have the laugh on her side; and don't be frightened by the idea of his acting more strictly up to the precepts of the New Testament than others. And now, my dear Fanny, having written so much on one side of the question, I shall turn round and entreat you not to commit yourself farther, and not to think of accepting him unless you really do like him. Anything is to be preferred or endured rather than marrying without Affection; and if his deficiencies of Manner etc. strike you more than all his good qualities, if you continue to think strongly of them, give him up at once.

Things are now in such a state, that you must resolve upon one or the other, either to allow him to go on as he has done, or whenever you are together behave with a coldness which may convince him that he has been deceiving himself. I have no doubt of his suffering a good deal for a time, a great deal, when he feels that he must give you up—but it is no creed of mine, as you must be well aware, that such sort of Disappointments kill anybody.

# PIERRE CURIE ASKS MARIE SKLODOVSKA TO MARRY HIM:
### ❦ *French scientist, 1859–1906* ❧

Nothing could have given me greater pleasure than to get news of you. The prospect of remaining two months without hearing about you had been extremely disagreeable to me: that is to say, your little note was more than welcome.

I hope you are laying up a stock of good air and that you will come back to us in October. As for me, I think I shall not go any-where; I shall stay in the country, where I spend the whole day in front of my open window or in the garden.

We have promised each other—haven't we?—to be at least great friends. If you will only not change your mind! For there are no promises that are binding; such things cannot be ordered at will. It would be a fine thing, just the same, in which I hardly dare believe, to pass our lives near each other, hypnotized by our dreams, your patriotic dream, our humanitarian dream, and our scientific dream.

Of all those dreams the last is, I believe, the only legitimate one. I mean by that that we are powerless to change the social order and, even if we were not, we should not know what to do; in taking action, no matter what direction, we should never be sure of not doing more harm than good, by retarding some inevitable evolution. From the scientific point of view, on the contrary, we may hope to do something; the ground is solider here, and any discovery that we may make, however small, will remain acquired knowledge.

See how it works out: it is agreed that we shall be great friends, but if you leave France in a year it would be an altogether too Platonic friendship, that of two creatures who would never see each other again. Wouldn't it be better for you to stay with me? I know that this question angers you, and that you don't want to speak of it again—and then, too, I feel so thoroughly unworthy of you from every point of view.

I thought of asking your permission to meet you by chance in Fribourg. But you are staying there, unless I am mistaken, only one day, and on that day you will of course belong to our friends the Kovalskis.

# KING SOLOMON TO HIS SON:
### ❧ *King of Israel, tenth century* B.C. ❧

My son, pay attention to my wisdom; lend your ear to my under-standing. That you may preserve discretion, and your lips may keep knowledge. For the lips of an immoral woman drip honey, and her mouth is smoother than oil; but in the end she is bitter as worm-wood, sharp as a two-edged sword. Her feet go down to death, her steps lay hold of hell. Lest you ponder her path of life—her ways are unstable; you do not know them.

    Therefore hear me now, my children, and do not depart from the words of my mouth. Remove your way far from her, and do not go near the door of her house, lest you give your honor to others, and your years to the cruel one; lest aliens be filled with your wealth, and your labors go to the house of a foreigner; and you mourn at last, when your flesh and your body are consumed, and say: " How I have hated instruction, and my heart despised correction! I have not obeyed the voice of my teachers, nor inclined my ear to those who instructed me! I was on the verge of total ruin, in the midst of the assembly and congregation."

Drink water from your own cistern, and running water from your own well. Should your fountains be dispersed abroad, streams of water in the streets? Let them be only your own, and not for strangers with you. Let your fountain be blessed, and rejoice with the wife of your youth. As a loving deer and a graceful doe, let her breasts satisfy you at all times; and always be enraptured with her love. For why should you, my son, be enraptured by an immoral woman, and be embraced in the arms of a seductress?

For the ways of man are before the eyes of the Lord, and He ponders all his paths. His own iniquities entrap the wicked man, and he is caught in the cords of his sin. He shall die for lack of instruction, and in the greatness of his folly he shall go astray.

---

THE APOSTLE PAUL TO THE CHRISTIANS
IN THE CITY OF CORINTH:
*Christian apostle and missionary, c. 10–65*

Though I speak with the tongues of men and of angels, and have not charity, I am become as sounding brass, or a tinkling cymbal. And though I have the gift of prophecy, and understand all mysteries, and all knowledge; and though I have all faith, so that I could remove mountains, and have not charity, I am nothing. And though I bestow all my goods to feed the poor, and though I give my body to be burned, and have not charity, it profiteth me nothing.

Charity suffereth long, and is kind; charity envieth not; charity vaunteth not itself, is not puffed up, doth not behave itself unseemly, seeketh not her own, is not easily provoked, thinketh no evil; rejoiceth not in iniquity, but rejoiceth in the truth; beareth all things, believeth all things, hopeth all things, endureth all things.

Charity never faileth: but whether there be prophecies, they shall fail; whether there be tongues, they shall cease; whether there be knowledge, it shall vanish away. For we know in part, and we prophesy in part. But when that which is perfect is come, then that which is in part shall be done away.

When I was a child, I spoke as a child, I understood as a child, I thought as a child: but when I became a man, I put away childish things.

For now we see through a glass, darkly; but then face to face: now I know in part; but then shall I know even as also I am known. And now abideth faith, hope, charity, these three; but the greatest of these is charity.

# SIR WALTER RALEIGH TO HIS WIFE A FEW HOURS BEFORE HE IS TO BE EXECUTED:

*English courtier, navigator, colonizer, and writer, c. 1552–1618*

You shall now receive (my deare wife) my last words in these my last lines. My love I send you that you may keep it when I am dead, and my councell that you may remember it when I am no more. I would not by my will present you with sorrowes (dear Besse) let them go to the grace with me and be buried in the dust. And seeing that it is not Gods will that I should see you any more in this life, beare it patiently, and with a heart like thy selfe.

First, I send you all the thankes which my heart can conceive, or my words can reherse for your many travailes, and care taken for me, which though they have not taken effect as you wished, yet my debt to you is not the lesse: but pay it I never shall in this world.

Secondly, I beseech you for the love you beare me living, do not hide your selfe many dayes, but by your travailes seeke to helpe our miserable fortunes and the right of your poor childe. Thy mourning cannot availe me, I am but dust.

Thirdly, you shall understand, that my land was conveyed bona fide to my childe: the writings were drawne at midsummer was twelve months, my honest cosen Brett can testify so much, and Dolberry too, can remember somewhat therein. And I trust my blood will quench their malice that have cruelly murthered me: and that they will not seek also to kill thee and thine with extreame poverty.

To what friend to direct thee I know not, for all mine have left me in the true time of tryall. And I perceive that my death was determined from the first day. Most sorry I am God knows that being thus surprised with death I can leave you in no better estate. God is my witnesse I meant you all my office of wines or all that I could have purchased by selling it, halfe of my stuffe, and all my jewels, but some one for the boy, but God hath prevented all my resolutions. That great God that ruleth all in all, but if you live free from want, care for no more, for the rest is but vanity. Love God, and begin betimes to repose your selfe upon him, and therein shall you finde true and lasting riches, and endlesse comfort: for the rest when you have travailed and wearied your thoughts over all sorts of worldly cogitations, you shall but sit downe by sorrowe in the end.

Teach your son also to love and feare God whilst he is yet young, that the feare of God may grow with him, and then God will be a husband to you, and a father to him; a husband and a father which cannot be taken from you.

Baily oweth me 200 pounds, and Adrian Gilbert 600. In Jersey I also have much owing me besides. The arrearages of the wines will pay my debts. And howsoever you do for my soles sake, pay all poore men. When I am gone, no doubt you shall be sought for by many, for the world thinkes that I was very rich. But take heed of the pretences of men, and their affections, for they last not but in honest and worthy men, and no greater misery can befall you in this life, than to become a prey, and afterwards to be despised. I spake not this (God knowes) to dissuade you from marriage, for it will be best for you, both in respect of the world and of God. As for me, I am no more yours, nor you mine, death hath cut us asunder: and God hath divided me from the world, and you from me.

Remember your poor childe for his father's sake, who chose you, and loved you in his happiest times. Get those letters (if it be possible) which I writ to the Lords, wherein I sued for my life: God is my witnesse it was for you and yours that I desired life, but it is true that I disdained my self for begging of it: for know it (my dear wife) that your son is the son of a true man, and one who in his owne respect despiseth death and all his misshapen and ugly formes.

I cannot write much, God he knows how hardly I steale this time while others sleep, and it is also time that I should separate my thoughts from the world. Begg my dead body which living was denied thee; and either lay it at Sherburne (and if the land continue) or in Exeter-Church, by my Father and Mother; I can say no more, time and death call me away.

The everlasting God, powerfull, infinite, and omnipotent God, That Almighty God, who is goodnesse it selfe, the true life and true light keep thee and thine: have mercy on me, and teach me to forgive my persecutors and false accusers, and send us to meet in his glorious Kingdome. My dear wife farewell. Blesse my poore boy. Pray for me, and let my good God hold you both in his armes.

Written with the dying hand of sometimes thy Husband, but now alasse overthrowne. Yours that was, but now not my own.

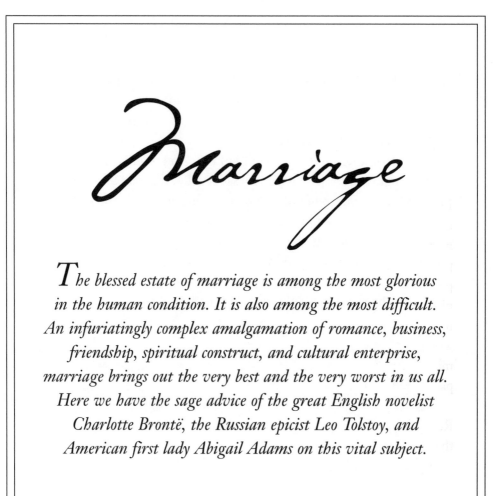

*Marriage*

*T*he blessed estate of marriage is among the most glorious
in the human condition. It is also among the most difficult.
*An infuriatingly complex amalgamation of romance, business,*
*friendship, spiritual construct, and cultural enterprise,*
*marriage brings out the very best and the very worst in us all.*
*Here we have the sage advice of the great English novelist*
*Charlotte Brontë, the Russian epicist Leo Tolstoy, and*
*American first lady Abigail Adams on this vital subject.*

# CHARLOTTE BRONTË TO HER FRIEND ELIZABETH GASKELL:

*English novelist, 1816–1855*

Do not be over-persuaded to marry a man you can never respect—I do not say love; because, I think, if you can respect a person before marriage, moderate love at least will come after; and as to intense passion, I am convinced that that is no desirable feeling. In the first place, it seldom or never meets with a requital; and, in the second place, if it did, the feeling would only be temporary: it would last the honeymoon, and then, perhaps, give place to disgust, or indifference worse, perhaps, than disgust. Certainly this would be the case on the man's part; and on the woman's—God help her, if she is left to love passionately and alone.

I am tolerably well convinced that I shall never marry at all. Reason tells me so, and I am not so utterly the slave of feeling but that I can occasionally hear her voice.

## LEO TOLSTOY TO HIS SON:

*Russian novelist and philosopher, 1828–1910*

The goal of our life should not be to find joy in marriage, but to bring more love and truth into the world. We marry to assist each other in this larger task. Though we should indeed love our spouse with true satisfaction, the most selfish and hateful life of all is that of two beings who unite merely in order to enjoy pleasures. The highest calling is that of the man who has dedicated his life to serving God and doing good, and who unites with a woman in order to happily further that purpose.

## ARNOLD CROMWELL TO HIS COUSIN:

*English journalist and playwright, 1897–1971*

To keep the fire burning brightly there is one easy rule: keep the two logs together, near enough to keep each other warm and far enough apart—about a finger's breadth—for breathing room. Good fire, good marriage, same rule.

# Abigail Adams to her husband John Adams:
### ◁ *First Lady of the United States, 1744–1818* ▷

I wish you would ever write me a Letter half as long as I write you; and tell me if you may where your fleet are gone? What sort of Defense Virginia can make against our common Enemy? Whether it is so situated as to make an able Defense? Are not the Gentry Lords and the common people vassals, are they not like the uncivilized Natives Britain represents us to be? I hope their Rifle Men who have shown themselves very savage and even Blood thirsty; are not a specimen of the Generality of the people.

I am willing to allow the Colony great merit for having produced a Washington but they have been shamefully duped by a Dunmore.

I have sometimes been ready to think that the passion for Liberty cannot be Equally Strong in the breasts of those who have been accustomed to deprive their fellow Creatures of theirs. Of this I am certain that it is not founded upon that generous and Christian principal of doing to others as we would that others should do unto us.

Do not you want to see Boston; I am fearful of the small pox, or I should have been in before this time. I got Mr. Crane to go to our House and see what state it was in. I find it has been occupied by one of the Doctors of a Regiment, very dirty, but no other damage has been done to it. The few things which were left in it are all gone. Cranch has the key to get it cleaned as soon as possible and shut it up. I look upon it a new acquisition of property, a property which one month ago did not value at a single Shilling, and could with pleasure have seen it in flames.

The Town in General is left in a better state than we expected, more owing to a precipitate flight than any Regard to the inhabitants, tho some individuals discovered a sense of honour and justice and have left the rent of the Houses in which they were, for the owners and the furniture unhurt, or if damaged sufficient to make it good.

Others have committed abominable Ravages. The Mansion House of your President is safe and the furniture unhurt whilst both the House and Furniture of the Solicitor General have fallen a prey to their own merciless party. Surely the very Fiends feel a Reverential awe for Virtue and patriotism, whilst they Detest the parricide and traitor.

I feel very differently at the approach of spring to what I did a month ago. We knew not then whether we could plant or sow with safety, whether when we had toiled we could reap the fruits of our own industry, whether we could rest in our own Cottages, or whether we should not be driven from the sea coasts to seek shelter in the wilderness, but now we feel as if we might sit under our own vine and eat the good of the land.

I feel a *gaieti de Coar* to which before I was a stranger. I think the Sun looks brighter, the birds sing more melodiously, and Nature puts on a more cheerful countenance. We feel a temporary peace, and the poor fugitives are returning to their deserted habitations.

Tho we felicitate ourselves, we sympathize with those who are trembling lest the lot of Boston should be theirs. But they cannot be in similar circumstances unless pusillanimity and cowardice should take possession of them. They have time and warning given them to see the Evil and shun it. I long to hear that you have declared an independancy—and by the way in the new Code of Laws which I suppose it will be necessary for you to make I desire you would Remember the Ladies, and be more generous and favorable to them than your ancestors. Do not put such unlimited power into the hands of the Husbands. Remember all Men would be tyrants if they could. If particular care and attention is not paid to the Ladies we are determined to foment a Rebellion, and will not hold ourselves bound by any Laws in which we have no voice, or Representation.

That your Sex are Naturally Tyrannical is a Truth so thoroughly established as to admit of not dispute, but such of you as wish to be happy willingly give up the harsh title of Master for the more tender and endearing one of Friend. Why then, not put it out of the power of the vicious and the Lawless to use us with cruelty and indignity with impunity. Men of Sense in all Ages abhor those customs which treat us only as the vassals of your Sex. Regard us then as beings placed by providence under your protection and in imitation of the Supreme Being make use of that power only for our happiness.

# Money

*Though it is true that the love of money is the root of all evil, it is also true that the lack of money is the root of much bitterness! Most of us live our lives camped precariously somewhere between both pitfalls. The tension is something that most of us never fully resolve. As a result we need all the financial advice we can get. Here we have the advantage of gleaning some such advice from the financier Bernard Baruch, from the Victorian novelist Charles Dickens, the incomparable Samuel Johnson, and several others.*

# CHARLES DICKENS TO HIS SON, HENRY:

*English novelist and journalist, 1812–1870*

I have your letter here this morning. I enclose you another cheque for twenty-five pounds, and I write to London by this post, ordering three dozen sherry, two dozen port, six bottles of brandy, and three dozen light claret, to be sent down to you. And I enclose a cheque in favor of the Rev. F. L. Hopkins for £5.10

Now, observe attentively. We must have no shadow of debt. Square up everything whatsoever that it has been necessary to buy. Let not a farthing be outstanding on any account, when we begin with your allowance. Be particular in the minutest detail.

I wish to have no secret from you in the relations we are to establish together, and I therefore send you Joe Chitty's letter bodily. Reading it, you will know exactly what I know, and will understand that I treat you with perfect confidence. It appears to me that an allowance of two hundred and fifty pounds a year will be handsome for all your wants, if I send you your wines. I mean this to include your tailor's bills as well as every other expense; and I strongly recommend you to buy nothing in Cambridge, and to take credit for nothing but the clothes with which your tailor provides you. As soon as you have got your furniture accounts in, let us wipe all those preliminary expenses clean out, and I will then send you your first quarter. We will count it in October, November, and December; and your second quarter will begin with the New Year If you dislike, at first, taking charge of so large a sum as sixty-two pounds ten shillings, you can have your money from me half-quarterly.

You know how hard I work for what I get, and I think you know that I never had money help from any human creature after I was a child. You know that you are one of many heavy charges on me, and that I trust to your so exercising your abilities and improving the advantages of your past expensive education, as soon to diminish *this* charge. I say no more on that head.

Whatever you do, above all other things keep out of debt and confide in me. If ever you find yourself on the verge of any perplexity or difficulty, come to me. You will never find me hard with you while you are manly and truthful.

As your brothers have gone away one by one, I have written to each of them what I am now going to write you. You know that you have never been hampered with religious forms of restraint, and that with mere unmeaning forms I have no sympathy. But I most strongly and affectionately impress upon you the priceless value of the

New Testament, and the study of that book as the one unfailing guide in life. Deeply respecting it, and bowing down before the character of our Saviour, as separated from the vain constructions and inventions of men, you cannot go very wrong, and will always preserve at heart a true spirit of veneration and humility. Similarly I impress upon you the habit of saying a Christian prayer every night and morning. These things have stood by me all through my life, and remember that I tried to render the New Testament intelligible to you and lovable by you when you were a mere baby. And so God bless you. Ever your affectionate Father.

---

SENATOR EVERETT DIRKSON TO HIS COLLEAGUES:
*Illinois senator, 1896–1969*

A billion here, a billion there—pretty soon it adds up to real money.

---

BERNARD BARUCH TO HIS YOUNG FRIEND, HERBERT STEIN:
*Financier and politician, 1870–1965*

Work and save.

### JAMES HILL TO A YOUNG EMPLOYEE:
*American railroad magnate, 1838–1916*

If you want to know whether you are destined to be a success or failure in life, you can easily find out. One test is simple and infallible. Are you able to save money? If not, drop out. You will lose.

---

### SAMUEL GOLDWYN TO DAVID STEIN:
*American film producer, 1882–1974*

Spare no expense to make everything as economical as possible.

---

### GERTRUDE STEIN TO ERNEST HEMINGWAY:
*American writer, 1874–1946*

Money is always there, but the pockets change.

# SAMUEL JOHNSON TO JAMES BOSWELL:

*English writer and lexicographer, 1709–1784*

Of law-suits there is no end; poor Sir Allan must have another trial, for which, however, his antagonist cannot be much blamed, having two judges on his side. I am more afraid of the debts than of the House of Lords. It is scarcely to be imagined to what debts will swell, that are daily increasing by small additions, and how carelessly in a state of desperation debts are contracted.

Poor Macquarry was far from thinking that when he sold his islands he should receive nothing. For what were they sold? And what was their yearly value? The admission of money into the Highlands will soon put an end to the feudal modes of life, by making those men landlords who were not chiefs. I do not know that the people will suffer by the change; but there was in the patriarchal authority something venerable and pleasing. Every eye must look with pain on a Campbell turning the Macquarries at will out of their sedes avitae, their hereditary island.

# KING SOLOMON TO HIS SON:

*King of Israel, Tenth century B.C.*

My son, if you become surety for your friend, if you have shaken hands in pledge for a stranger, you are snared by the words of your mouth; you are taken by the words of your mouth. So do this, my son, and deliver yourself; for you have come into the hand of your friend: go and humble yourself; plead with your friend. Give no sleep to your eyes, nor slumber to your eyelids. Deliver yourself like a gazelle from the hand of the hunter, and like a bird from the hand of the fowler.

Go to the ant, you sluggard! Consider her ways and be wise, which, having no captain, overseer or ruler, provides her supplies in the summer, and gathers her food in the harvest. How long will you slumber, O sluggard? When will you rise from your sleep? A little sleep, a little slumber, a little folding of the hands to sleep—so shall your poverty come on you like a prowler, and your need like an armed man.

# REV. EDWARD PAYSON TO A CHRISTIAN BROTHER
## OF RANK AND WEALTH:
*American pastor, 1783–1827*

I have thought much of your situation since I left you. It is but seldom that God gives one of his children so many temporal blessings as he has given you. He has hitherto preserved you, and will, I trust, continue to preserve you from the evils which attend a state of prosperity. But it is, as you are aware, a dangerous state, and calls for great watchfulness and much prayer. You are, doubtless, conscious of many evil propensities working within; but they may work long, and produce much internal mischief before their effects become external and visible to others.

The effects of temporal prosperity upon the mind resemble those of an unhealthy atmosphere upon the body. The constitution is gradually and almost insensibly undermined and weakened; and yet no particular part can be pointed out as the seat of the disease, for the poison is diffused through the whole system. Spiritual lassitude, the loss of spiritual appetite, and an indisposition to vigorous spiritual exertion, are some of the first perceptible symptoms that the poison of prosperity is at work. When a man detects these symptoms in himself, it is time for him to be alarmed. If he delays a little longer, the disease will make such progress and to render him insensible to his danger.

Were I placed in such a situation I should be ruined in six months. Still, your situation is, in one respect, desirable. It is one in which you may do much for the glory of God and the promotion of his cause.

---

### SAMUEL JOHNSON TO JAMES BOSWELL:
*English writer and lexicographer, 1709–1784*

You are only poor when you want more than you have.

*Reading*

*Even in the time of Solomon it could be said that "of the making of books there is no end." So rich is the companionship of books, so profound is the enrichment of books, and so deep is the pleasure of books that none of the vast changes in cultures and civilizations since has stemmed their ever-rising tide. The following letters show just why. Whether extolling the virtues of collecting a personal library as in the case of Henry Ward Beecher, examining the relative merits of fiction as in the case of Theodore Roosevelt, or recommending actual volumes as in the case of Thomas Jefferson, each of these letters evinces a bibliophilism not uncommon to Western Civilization's best and brightest.*

# ANTHONY TROLLOPE TO HIS PUBLISHER:

*English novelist, 1815–1882*

This habit of reading, I make bold to tell you, is your pass to the greatest, the purest, and the most perfect pleasures that God has prepared for His creatures. It lasts when all other pleasures fade.

---

# CICERO TO A YOUNG PUPIL:

*Roman statesman, orator, and philosopher, 106–43 B.C.*

Books are the food of youth; the delight of old age; the ornament of prosperity; the refuge and comfort of adversity; a delight at home; no hindrance abroad; companions at night, in traveling, in the country. Indeed, no wise man ought ever be found apart their company.

Books are the wise man's passport to success and greatness. Books are the thresholds to wonder; the gateways to enlightenment; the foundations of virtue; and the pediment of honor.

Read at every wait; read at all hours; read within leisure; read about in times of labor; read as one goes in; read as one goes out. The task of the educated mind is simply put: read to lead.

## THOMAS CARLYLE TO HIS WIFE JANE:
*Scottish historian and essayist, 1795–1881*

No book that will not improve by repeated readings deserves to be read at all.

---

## HENRY WARD BEECHER TO HIS FRIEND JOSHUA CARSON:
*American pastor and newspaper editor, 1813–1887*

A little library, growing every year, is an honorable part of a man's history. It is a man's duty to have books. A library is not a luxury, but one of the necessaries of life. Be certain that your house is adequately and properly furnished—with books rather than with furniture. Both if you can, but books at any rate.

# THEODORE ROOSEVELT TO HIS SON KERMIT:

*American author, adventurer, and president, 1858–1919*

I sympathize with every word you say in your letter, about Nicholas Nickleby, and about novels generally. Normally I only care for a novel if the ending is good, and I quite agree with you that if the hero has to die he ought to die worthily and nobly, so that our sorrow at the tragedy shall be tempered with the joy and pride one always feels when a man does his duty well and bravely. There is quite enough sorrow and shame and suffering and baseness in real life, and there is no need for meeting it unnecessarily in fiction.

As Police Commissioner it was my duty to deal with all kinds of squalid misery and hideous and unspeakable infamy, and I should have been worse than a coward if I had shrunk from doing what was necessary; but there would have been no use whatever in my reading novels detailing all this misery and squalor and crime, or at least in reading them as a steady thing.

Now and then there is a powerful but sad story which really is interesting and which really does good; but normally the books which do good and the books which healthy people find interesting are those which are not in the least of the sugar-candy variety, but which, while portraying foulness and suffering when they must be portrayed, yet have a joyous as well as a noble side.

# THOMAS JEFFERSON TO HIS NEPHEW ROBERT SKIPWITH:

*American patriot, scientist, and president, 1743–1826*

I sat down with a design of executing your request to form a catalogue of books amounting to about £30 Sterling. But could by no means satisfy myself with any partial choice I could make. Thinking therefore it might be as agreeable to you, I have framed such a general collection as I think you would wish, and might in time find convenient, to procure. Out of this you will choose for yourself to the amount you mentioned for the present year, and may hereafter as shall be convenient proceed in completing the whole.

A view of the second column in this catalogue would I suppose extort a smile from the face of gravity. Peace to its wisdom! Let me not awaken it. A little attention however to the nature of the human mind evinces that the entertainments of fiction are useful as well as pleasant. That they are pleasant when well written, every person feels who reads. But wherein is its utility, ask the reverend sage, big with the notion that nothing can be useful but the learned lumber of Greek and Roman reading with which his head is stored? I answer, every thing is useful which contributes to fix us in the principles and practice of virtue.

When any signal act of charity or of gratitude, for instance, is presented either to our sight or imagination, we are deeply impressed with its beauty and feel a strong desire in ourselves of doing charitable and grateful acts also. On the contrary when we see or read of any atrocious deed, we are disgusted with its deformity and conceive an abhorrence of vice.

Now every emotion of this kind is an exercise of our virtuous dispositions; and dispositions of the mind, like limbs of the body, acquire strength by exercise. But exercise produces habit; and in the instance of which we speak, the exercise being of the moral feelings, produces a habit of thinking and acting virtuously. We never reflect whether the story we read be truth or fiction. If the painting be lively, and a tolerable picture of nature, we are thrown into a reverie, from which if we awaken it is the fault of the writer. I appeal to every reader of feeling and sentiment whether the fictitious murder of Duncan by Macbeth in Shakespeare does not excite in him as great horror of villainy, as the real one of Henry IV by Ravaillac as related Davila? And whether the fidelity of Nelson, and generosity of Blandford in Marmontel do not dilate his breast, and elevate his sentiments as much as any similar incident which real history can furnish? Does he not in fact feel himself a better man while reading them, and privately covenant to copy the fair example? We neither know nor care whether Lawrence Sterne really went to France, whether he was there accosted by the poor Franciscan, at first rebuked him unkindly, and then gave him a peace offering; or whether the whole be not a fiction. In either case we are equally sorrowful at the rebuke, and secretly resolve we will never do so: we are pleased with the subsequent atonement, and view with emulation a soul candidly acknowledging its fault, and making a just reparation.

Considering history as a moral exercise, her lessons would be too infrequent if confined to real life. Of those recorded by historians few incidents have been attended with such circumstances as to excite in any high degree this sympathetic emotion of virtue. We are therefore wisely framed to be as warmly interested for a fictitious as for a real personage. The spacious field of imagination is thus laid open to our use, and lessons may be formed to illustrate and carry home to the mind every moral rule of life. Thus a lively and lasting sense of filial duty is more effectually impressed on the mind of a son or daughter by reading King Lear, than by all the dry volumes of ethics and divinity that ever were written. This is my idea of well-written Romance, of Tragedy, Comedy, and Epic Poetry.

If you are fond of speculation, the books under the head of

Criticism, will afford you much pleasure. Of Politicks and Trade I have given you a few only of the best books, as you would probably choose to be not unacquainted with those commercial principles which bring wealth into our country, and the constitutional security we have for the enjoyment of that wealth.

In Law I mention a few systematical books, as a knowledge of the minutiae of that science is not necessary for a private gentleman. In Religion, History, Natural philosophy, I have followed the same plan in general.

But whence the necessity of this collection? Come to the new Rowanty, from which you may reach your hand to a library formed on a more extensive plan. Separated from each other but a few paces, the possessions of each would be open to the other. A spring, centrically situated, might be the scene of every evening's joy. There we should talk over the lessons of the day, or lose them in Musick, Chess, or the merriments of our family companions. The heart thus lightened, our pillows would be soft, and health and long life would attend the happy scene.

Come then and bring our dear Tibby with you; the first in your affections, and second in mine. Offer prayers for me too at that shrine to which, tho' absent, I pay continual devotion. In every scheme of happiness she is placed in the foreground of the picture, as the principal figure. Take that away, and it is no picture for me. Bear my affections to Wintipock, clothed in the warmest expressions of sincerity; and to yourself be every human felicity.

FINE ARTS
*Observations on Gardening* by
   Payne
Webb's *Essay on Painting*
Homer's *Odyssey*
Dryden's translation of
   Virgil
Milton's Works
Hoole's *Tasso*
Ossian with Blair's Criticisms
*Telemachus* by Dodsley
Capell's Shakespeare
Dryden's Plays
Addison's Plays
Otway's Plays
Rowe's Works

Thompson's Works
Young's Works
Home's Plays
Mallet's Works
Mason's Poetical Works
Terence's Works
Moliere's Works
Farquhar's Works
Steele's Works
Congreve's Works
Garric's Dramatic Works
Foote's Dramatic Works
Rousseau's *Eloisa*
Rousseau's *Emilius and Sophia*
Marmontel's *Moral Tales*
*Gil Blas* translated by Smollet

*Don Quixote* translated by
   Smollet
David Simple's Works
Smollet's *Roderic Random*
Smollet's *Peregrine Pickle*
Smollet's *Launcelot Graces*
Smollet's *Adventures of a Ginea*
Richardson's *Pamela*
Richardson's *Clarissa*
Richardson's *Grandison*
Richardson's *Fool of Quality*
Feilding's Works
Langhorne's *Constantia*
Langhorne's *Solyan and Almena*
Goldsmith's *Vicar of Wakefield*
Percy's *Runic Poems*
Percy's *Reliques of Ancient
   English Poetry*
Percy's *Han Kiou Chouan*
Percy's *Miscellaneous Chinese
   Pieces*

Chaucer's Complete Works
Spencer's Complete Works
Waller's Poems
Dodsley's Collection of Poems
Pearch's Collection of Poems
Gray's Works
Ogilvie's Poems
Prior's Poems
Gay's Works
Shenstone's Works
Dryden's Works
Pope's Works collected by
   Warburton
Churchill's Poems
Swift's Works
Swift's Literary Correspondence
Addison and Steele's *Spectator*
*Tatler*
*Guardian*
*Freeholder*
Lord Lyttleton's *Persian Letters*

CRITICISM on the
FINE ARTS
Lord Kaim's *Elements of*
*Criticism*
Burke *On the Sublime and*
*Beautiful*
Hogarth's *Analysis of Beauty*
Reid *On the Human Mind*
Smith's *Theory of Moral*
*Sentiments*
Johnson's *Dictionary*
Capell's *Polusions*

POLITICKS
Montesquieu's *Spirit of Laws*
Locke *On Government*
Sidney *On Government*
Marmontel's *Belisarius*
Lord Bolingbroke's Political
Works
Montesquieu's *Rise and Fall of*
*the Roman Government*

Stuart's *Political Economy*
Petty's *Political Arithmetic*

METAPHYSIKS and
PHILOSOPHY
Locke's *Conduct of the Mind in*
*Search of Truth*
Xenophon's *Memoirs of*
*Socrates*
*Epictetus* by Mrs. Carter
*Antonius* by Collins
*Seneca* by L'Estrange
Cicero's *Offices* by Guthrie
Cicero's *Tusculan Questions*
Lord Bolingbroke's
Philosophical Works
Hume's Essays
Lord Kaim's *Natural Religion,*
*Philosophical Survey of*
*Nature, Economy of Human*
*Life*
Sterne's *Sermons*
Sherlock *On Death*
Sherlock *On a Future State*

## LAW

Lord Kaim's *Principles of
  Equity*
Blackstone's *Commentaries*
Cuningham's *Law Dictionary*

## ANCIENT HISTORY

Bible
Rollin's *Ancient History*
Stanyan's *Graecian History*
Livy's Works
*Sallust* by Gordon
*Tacitus* by Gordon
Josephus *History of the War*
Vertot's *Revolutions of
  Rome*
Plutarch's *Lives* translated
  by Langhorne
Bayle's *Dictionary*
Jeffrey's *Historical &
  Chronological Chart*

## MODERN HISTORY

Robertson's *History of Charles
  the V*$^{th}$
Bossuet's *History of France*
*Davila* by Farneworth
Hume's *History of England*
Clarendon's *History of the
  Rebellion*
Robertson's *History of Scotland*
Keiths *History of Virginia*
Stith's *History of Virginia*

## NATURAL PHILOSOPHY
  and NATURAL HISTORY

Franklin *On Electricity*
Macqueer's *Elements of
  Chemistry*
Home's *Principles of Agriculture*
Tull's *Horse-Hoeing Husbandry*
Duhamel's *Husbandry*
Millar's *Gardener's Dictionary*

Buffon's *Natural History*
*A Compendium of Physic &*
 *Surgery* by Nourse
Addison's *Travels*
Anson's *Voyage*
Thompson's *Travels*
Lady M. W. Montague's
 *Letters*

MISCELLANEOUS
Lord Lyttleton's *Dialogues of*
 *the Dead*
Fenelon's *Dialogues of the Dead*
Voltaire's Works
Locke *On Education*
Owens *Dictionary of Arts &*
 *Sciences*

These books if bound quite plain will cost the prices affixed in this catalogue. If bound elegantly, gilt, lettered, and marbled on the leaves, they will cost 20 percent more. If bound by Bumgarden in fine Marbled bindings, they will cost 50 percent more. Adieu.

# FULWAR SKIPWITH TO HIS COUSIN ROBERT SKIPWITH IN RESPONSE TO JEFFERSON'S LETTER:
*President of the Republic of West Florida, 1749–1811*

Hearing of our esteemed uncle's recommendations for a gentleman's proper library, I could not but help to desire emendations upon several issues. Though his selections show an the obvious felicity of mind from a lifetime of study, they also evidence peculiar biases, particularly in the questions of orthodox religion and the conduct of Western Christendom.

I therefore humbly offer these essential volumes for due consideration in your enterprise.

## OVERVIEW CLASSICISM
Aristotle's *Rhetoric*
Aristotle's *Poetics*
Breatton's *Mythology*
Homer's *Illiad*
Plato's *Republic*

## SURVEY PATRISTISM
Athanasius's *On the Incarnation*
Augustine's *Confessions*
Augustine's *The City of God*
Malory's *Le Mort d'Arthur*
Joinville's *Chronicles of the Crusades*
Villehardouin's *Chronicles of the Crusades*

## RENAISSANCE PRACTICUM

Dante's *Inferno*
Erasmus's *In Praise of Folly*
Machiavelli's *Prince*
Vasari's *Lives of the Artists*

## REFORMATION THEOLOGY

Bunyan's *Pilgrim's Progress*
Calvin's *Institutes*
Knox's *History of the Reformation in Scotland*
Luther's *Bondage of the Will*
*Westminster Confession of Faith*

## MODERN SOCIAL CRITICISM

Johnson's *Lives of the Poets*
Johnson's *Rasselas*
More's *Utopia*
Rousseau's *The Social Contract*
Spenser's *The Fairie Queen*
Burke's *Reflections on the Revolution in France*
Cromwell's *Speeches*

May these works bless your home and adorn your life as they have so many generations before you. *Momento Mori.*

## Lyman Abbott to his friend Frederick Cooper:

*American pastor, writer, and editor, 1835–1922*

A broad interest in books usually means a broad interest in life.

---

## Oliver Wendell Holmes to his daughter:

*American physician and writer, 1809–1894*

It is a good plan to have a book with you in all places and at all times.

---

## Charles Spurgeon to his brother James:

*English author and pastor, 1834–1892*

The devil is not afraid of a dust-covered Bible.

## LORD BYRON TO HIS LOVE INTEREST, ALICE GRUMMERE:
*❦ English poet, 1788–1824 ❧*

But words are things, and a small drop of ink, falling like dew, upon a thought, produces that which makes thousands, perhaps millions, think.

---

## CHARLES LAMB TO HAROLD UNWIN:
*❦ English critic and essayist, 1775–1834 ❧*

I own that I am disposed to say grace upon twenty other occasions in the course of the day besides my dinner; why have we none for books?

# Relatives

*Kith and kin afford us both our greatest joys and our greatest heartaches. Especially when marriage doubles the number of our relations, special skills and particular disciplines are necessary to make such intimacies harmonious. Here it matters little if one is the Holy Roman Emperor Charlemagne or the English wit G.K. Chesterton, the dilemmas and challenges are the same.*

## CHARLEMAGNE THE GREAT TO CUTHBERT OF ORLEANS:
*King of the Franks and Holy Roman Emperor, 742–814*

Right relations within the extension of family at court I find to be the most plaguing of dilemmas and the most intriguing of concerns. A wife's mother can be a fierce adversary. Wise is the prince or courtesan who quickly offers fealty to the just causes she represents. For harmony throughout the kingdom, harmony within the home is a first requisite.

# G.K. CHESTERTON TO HIS FIANCÉE FRANCES BLOGG:
### ❧ *English poet, novelist, and essayist, 1874–1936* ❧

You say you want to talk to me about death: my views about death are bright, brisk and entertaining. When Azrael takes a soul it may be to other and brighter worlds: like those whither you and I go together. The transformation called Death may be something as beautiful and dazzling as the transformation called Love. It may make the dead man 'happy', just as you mother knows that you are happy. But none the less it is a transformation, and sad sometimes for those left behind. A mother whose child is dying can hardly believe that in the inscrutable Unknown there is anyone who can look to it as well as she. And if a mother cannot trust her child easily to God Almighty, shall I be so mean as to be angry because she cannot trust it easily to me?

I tell you I have stood before your mother and felt like a thief. I know you are not going to part: neither physically, mentally, morally nor spiritually. But she sees a new element in your life, wholly from outside—is it not natural, given her temperament, you should find her perturbed? Oh, dearest, dearest Frances, let us always be very gentle to older people. Indeed, darling, it is not they who are the tyrants, but we. They may interrupt our building in the scaffolding stages we turn their house upside down when it is their final home and rest.

Your mother would certainly have worried if you had been engaged to the Archangel Michael (who, indeed, is bearing his disappointment very well): how much more when you are engaged to an aimless, tactless, reckless, unbrushed, strange-hatted, opinionated scarecrow who has suddenly walked into the vacant place. I could have prophesied her unrest: wait and she will calm down all right, dear. God comfort her: I dare not.

# Sport

*Throughout history sport has played a vital role in human relations. But like any good thing it has been misused and abused—given an importance all out of proportion to its true significance. Here the Apostle Paul, Supreme Court Justice Earl Warren, and President Theodore Roosevelt all reflect on the thrill of victory and the agony of defeat. In so doing they offer wise counsel on the appropriate priority and place of sport in our lives.*

# THE APOSTLE PAUL TO HIS YOUNG DISCIPLE TIMOTHY:

*Christian apostle and missionary, c. 10–65*

Bodily exercise profits a little, but godliness is profitable for all things having promise for the life that now is and of that which is to come.

---

# THEODORE ROOSEVELT TO HIS SON TED:

*American author, adventurer, and president, 1858–1919*

In spite of the "Hurry! Hurry!" on the outside of your envelope, I did not like to act until I had consulted Mother and thought the matter over; and to be frank with you, old fellow, I am by no means sure that I am doing right now. If it were not that I feel you will be so bitterly disappointed, I would strongly advocate your acquiescing in the decision to leave you off the second squad this year. I am proud of your pluck, and I greatly admire football—though it was not a game I was ever able to play myself, my qualities resembling your brother Kermit's rather than yours.

But the very things that make it a good game make it a rough game, and there is always the chance of your being laid up. Now, I should not in the least object to your being laid up for a season if you were striving for something worth while, to get on the Groton school team, for instance, or on your class team when you entered Harvard—for of course I don't think you will have the weight to entitle you to try for the varsity. But I am by no means sure that it is worth your while to run the risk of being laid up for the sake of playing in the second squad when you are a fourth former, instead of when you are a fifth former. I do not know that the risk is balanced by the reward. However, I have told the Rector that as you feel so strongly about it, I think that the chance of your damaging yourself in body is outweighed by the possibility of bitterness of spirit if you could not play.

Understand me, I should think mighty little of you if you permitted chagrin to make you bitter on some point where it was evidently right for you to suffer the chagrin. But in this case I am uncertain, and I shall give you the benefit of the doubt. If, however, the coaches at any time come to the conclusion that you ought not to be in the second squad, why you must come off without grumbling.

I am delighted to have you play football. I believe in rough, manly sports. But I do not believe in them if they degenerate into the sole end of anyone's existence. I don't want you to sacrifice standing well in your studies to any over-athleticism; and I need not tell you that character counts for a great deal more than either intellect or body in winning success in life. Athletic proficiency is a mighty good servant, and like so many other good servants, a mighty bad master.

Did you ever read Pliny's letter to Trajan, in which he speaks of its being advisable to keep the Greeks absorbed in athletics, because it distracted their minds from all serious pursuits, including soldiering, and prevented their ever being dangerous to the Romans? I have not a doubt that the British officers in the Boer War had their efficiency partly reduced because they had sacrificed their legitimate duties to an inordinate and ridiculous love of sports. A man must develop his physical prowess up to a certain point; but after he has reaches that point there are other things that count more.

In my regiment nine-tenths of the men were better horsemen than I was, while on the average they were certainly hardier and more enduring. Yet after I had had them a very short while they all knew, and I knew too, that nobody else could command them as I could. I am glad you should play football; I am glad that you should box; I am glad that you should ride and shoot and walk and row as well as you do. I should be very sorry if you did not do these things. But don't ever get into the frame of mind which regards these things as constituting the end to which all your energies must be devoted, or even the major portion of your energies.

---

# E ARL WARREN TO RICHARD NIXON:

*American jurist, chief justice of the U.S. Supreme Court, 1891–1974*

I always turn to the sports pages first, which record human achievements. The front pages have nothing but human failures.

*Tact*

*Manners are not intended to make us look good; they are almost entirely for the benefit of others. Politeness is the honor we bestow upon others. It is a recognition of the integrity of those around us. Likewise, tact is the respect we pay to others. It is a mark of genuine kindness and civil concourse. Here several sages, from Judith Martin—best known as Miss Manners—to the nineteenth-century physician and author Oliver Wendell Holmes, extol the value of such virtue.*

### JUDITH MARTIN TO HOWARD RIEFF:
*American author and etiquette expert, 1946–*

If you can't be kind, at least be vague.

---

### OLIVER WENDELL HOLMES TO HIS SON:
*American physician and writer, 1809–1894*

The nearer you come in relation with a person, the more necessary do tact and courtesy become.

---

### KEN HIBBARD TO CHARESE DALEY:
*American humorist, 1921–1988*

A never-failing way to get rid of a fellow is to tell him something for his own good.

# Margot Asquith to her young friend Winston Churchill:
### *English socialite, 1865–1945*

The fact is dear Winston (I am the most genuine woman in the world and I know from our talk you will excuse my frankness) you have a unique opportunity of improving your position in the eyes of the best element both in politics and society. Believe me cheap scores, hen-roost phrases, and all oratorical want of dignity is out of date.

You have only to say to yourself "Margot Asquith is a little boring and over-earnest but she is right. Loyalty, reserve and character pays more than all the squibs and crackers. I have got a beautiful young wife, an affectionate heart and love of amusement. I will make the Court, the Colonies, the West and the East end of London change their whole views of me. I shall thrive on being liked instead of loving abusive notice and rotten notoriety." Do this and you do well, my friend.

## GEORGE MAPIR TO HIS BROTHER WILLIAM MAPIR:
*Hungarian politician and philosopher, 1844–1929*

Never tell a lie, but the truth you don't always have to tell either. When you must shoot an arrow of truth, dip its point in honey.

---

## REV. JOHN WATSON TO HIS STUDENTS AT YALE UNIVERSITY:
*Scottish author and pastor, 1838–1907*

When a speaker is pleading a great cause, and sees hard-headed men glaring before them with such ferocity that every one knows they are afraid of breaking down, let him stop in the middle of a paragraph and take the collection, and if he be declaring the Evangel, and a certain tenderness comes over the faces of the people, let him close his words to them and call them to prayer. Speech can be too lengthy, too formal, too eloquent, too grammatical. For one to lose his toilsome introduction, in which he happened to mention two Germans, with quotations, and his twice-written conclusion, in which he had that pretty fancy from Tennyson, is hard to flesh and blood. But in those sacrifices of self the preacher's strength lies, on them the blessing of God rests.

## PRINCESS JULIA STUART TO HER DAUGHTER:
*⊰ Modern pretender to the Stuart line, 1941– ⊱*

Never underestimate the power of simple courtesy. Your courtesy may not be returned or remembered, but discourtesy will.

---

## WINSTON CHURCHILL TO HIS SON RANDOLPH:
*⊰ English author, statesman, and prime minister, 1874–1965 ⊱*

Tact is the unsaid part of what you think.

# Temptation

There is no escaping temptation. It confronts us with a dogged persistence at nearly every turn. But though it is omni-present, it is by no means omni-potent. The wise have learned of its wiles and discerned its subtleties. They have found the means to muster resistance. Here fellow travelers in the paths of temptation as widely divergent as might be imagined—from the gallant Stuart pretender to the English crown Bonnie Prince Charlie to the Emperor Napoleon, from the nineteenth-century inspirational writer Elizabeth Printiss to the brilliant physicist Albert Einstein—express the certainty that it may be, indeed, must be, subdued and defeated.

# E

ELIZABETH PRENTISS TO A FRIEND FOLLOWING A TIME
OF FIERCE TRIAL AND TEMPTATION:

*American novelist and hymn writer, 1818–1878*

I want to give you emphatic warning that you were never in such danger in your life. This is the language of bitter, bitter experience and is not mine alone. Leighton says the great Pirate lets the empty ships go by and robs the full ones. I do hope you will go on your way rejoicing, unto the perfect day. Hold on to Christ with your teeth if your hands get crippled; He, alone, is stronger than Satan; He, alone, knows all "sore temptations" mean.

# GEORGE WASHINGTON DECLINES THE OFFER OF A CROWN FROM THE THIRTEEN COLONIES:
### *American patriot, planter, and president, 1732–1799*

With a mixture of great surprise and astonishment I have read with attention the Sentiments you have submitted to my perusal. Be assured Sir, no occurrence in the course of the War, has given me more painful sensations than your information of there being such ideas existing in the Army as you have expressed and I must view with abhorrence, and reprehend with severity. For the present, the communication of them will rest in my own bosom, unless some further agitation of the matter shall make a disclosure necessary.

I am much at a loss to conceive what part of my conduct could have given encouragement to an address which to me seems big with the greatest mischiefs that can befall my Country. If I am not deceived in the knowledge of myself, you could not have found a person to whom your schemes are more disagreeable—at the same time in justice to my own feeling I must add, that no man possesses a more sincere wish to see ample justice done to the Army than I do, and as far as my powers and influence, in a constitution, may extend, they shall be employed to the utmost of my abilities to effect it, should there be any occasion.

Let me conjure you then, if you have any regard for your Country, concern for yourself or posterity, or respect for me, to banish these thoughts from your mind, and never communicate, as from yourself, or any one else, a sentiment of the like nature.

---

## BONNIE PRINCE CHARLIE TO LORD HAMILTON:
*Heir to the Stuart crown of Britain, 1720–1788*

The wages of sin are underreported and the pangs of temptation are underestimated.

---

## NAPOLEON TO HIS WIFE JOSEPHINE:
*French emperor, 1769–1821*

One may go wrong in many directions, but right in only one.

# ALBERT EINSTEIN TO ONE OF HIS STUDENTS, BETSY MORROW:
*German-born American theoretical physicist, 1879–1955*

He who would not eat forbidden fruit must stay away from the forbidden tree.

---

# HORACE GREELEY TO JAMES PEMBERTON:
*American journalist and politician, 1811–1872*

Some temptations come to the industrious; all temptations come to the idle.

---

# CHARLES SPURGEON TO HIS SON THOMAS:
*English author and pastor, 1834–1892*

Every temptation is an opportunity to flee to God.

# *Trials*

*T*he thickest clouds of woe often yield the freshest showers of blessing. But that is only evident in hindsight. When undergoing trials of various kinds it is more than a little difficult to count it all joy. Here the great composer Ludwig van Beethoven, the English apologist C.S. Lewis, and the masterful American novelist Herman Melville all deal with the problem of pain with substance and grace.

### HERMAN MELVILLE TO HIS DAUGHTER:
*American adventurer and novelist, 1819–1891*

To scale great heights, we must come out of the lowermost depths. The way to heaven is through hell.

---

### J.C. RYLE TO HIS YOUNG DEACON GILES RIVLETT:
*English author and pastor, 1816–1900*

Often the same thing that makes one person bitter makes another better.

---

### C.S. LEWIS TO JOY DAVIDMAN:
*British writer and critic, 1898–1963*

Affliction often prepares an ordinary person for an extraordinary destiny.

# LUDWIG VAN BEETHOVEN ADMITS HIS DEAFNESS TO HIS BROTHERS KARL AND JOHANN:
*German composer, 1770–1827*

O ye men, who think or say that I am malevolent, stubborn, or mis-anthropic, how greatly do ye wrong me, you do not know the secret causes of my seeming, from childhood my heart and mind were dis-posed to the gentle feeling of good will, I was even ever eager to accomplish great deeds, but reflect now that for 6 years I have been in a hopeless case, aggravated by senseless physicians, cheated year after year in the hope of improvement, finally compelled to face the prospect of a lasting malady (whose cure will take years, or, perhaps, be impossible), born with an ardent and lively temperament, even susceptible to the diversions of society, I was compelled early to iso-late myself, to live in loneliness, when I at times tried to forget all this, O how harshly was I repulsed by the doubly sad experience of my bad hearing, and yet it was impossible for me to say to men speak louder, shout, for I am deaf.

Ah how could I possibly admit an infirmity in the one sense which should have been more perfect in me than in others, a sense which I once possessed in highest perfection, a perfection such as few surely in my profession enjoy or ever have enjoyed. O I cannot do it, therefore forgive me when you see me draw back when I would gladly mingle with you, my misfortune is doubly painful because it must lead to my being misunderstood, for me there can be no recreation in society of my fellows, refined intercourse, mutual exchange of thought, only just as little as the greatest needs command may I mix with society.

I must live like an exile, if I approach near to people a hot terror seizes upon me, a fear that I may be subjected to the danger of letting my condition be observed—thus it has been during the last half year which I spent in the country, commanded by my intelligent physician to spare my hearing as much as possible, in this almost meting my present natural disposition, although I sometimes ran counter to it, yielding to my inclination for society, but what a humiliation when one stood beside me and heard a flute in the distance and I heard nothing, or someone heard the shepherd singing and again I heard nothing, such incidents brought me to the verge of despair, but little more and I would have put an end to my life—only art if was that withheld me, ah, it seemed impossible to leave the world until I had produced all that I felt called upon to produce, and so I endured this wretched existence—truly wretched, an excitable body which a sudden change can throw from the best into the worst state—patience—it is said I must now choose for my guide, I have done so, I hope my determination will remain firm to endure until it pleases the inexorable Parcae to break the thread, perhaps I shall get better perhaps not, I am prepared.

Forced already in my 28th year to become a philosopher, O it is not easy, less easy for the artist than for anyone else—Divine One lookest into my inmost soul, thou knowest it, thou knowest that love of man and desire to do good live therein. O men, when some day you read these words, reflect that ye did me wrong and let the unfortunate one comfort himself and find one of his kind who despite all the obstacles of nature yet did all that was in his power to be accepted among worthy artists and men. You my brothers Karl and Johann as soon as I am dead if Dr. Schmid is still alive ask him in my name to describe my malady and attach this document to the history of my illness so that so far as is possible at least the world may become reconciled with me after my death. At the same time I declare you two to the heirs to my small fortune (if so it can be called), divide it fairly, bear with and help each other, what injury you have done me you know was long ago forgiven.

To you brother Karl I give special thanks for the attachment you have displayed toward me of late. It is my wish that your lives may be better and freer from care than I have had, recommend virtue to your children, it alone can give happiness, not money, I speak from experience, it was virtue that upheld me in misery, to it next to my art I owe the fact that I did not end my life by suicide.

Farewell and love each other—I thank all my friends, particularly Prince Lichnowsky and Professor Schmid—I desire that the instruments from Prince L. be preserved by one of you but let no quarrel result from this, so soon as they can serve you a better purpose sell them, how glad will I be if I can still be helpful to you in my grave—with joy I hasten toward death—if it comes before I shall have had an opportunity to show all my artistic capacities it will still come too early for me despite my hard fate and I shall probably wish that it had come later—but even then I am satisfied, will it not free me from a state of endless suffering? Come when thou wilt I shall meet thee bravely. Farewell and do not wholly forget me when I am dead. I deserve this of you in having often in life thought of you, how to make you happy, be so.

## ISAAC WATTS TO KARL TANNEHAUSEN:

*❧ English poet, theologian, and hymn writer, 1674–1748 ❧*

A smooth sea never made a successful sailor. God often digs the wells of joy with the spades of affliction.

---

## CHARLES SPURGEON TO HIS SON THOMAS:

*❧ English author and pastor, 1834–1892 ❧*

All sunshine and no rain makes a desert.

# Work

*The* word "easy" *appears only once in the New Testament, and then in connection with the yoke. It is not surprising then that all matters worth anything at all demand of us a certain measure of labor and intensity. And though this might appear at first glance to be a plight of woe and hardship, it is in fact a part of the glory of the human experience. The Protestant reformer Martin Luther, the industrialist Malcolm Forbes, the Puritan Hugh Latimer, the American pioneer Cotton Mather, and the student Andy Tant all bear the same good news: work is good.*

# WARNIE LEWIS TO HIS BROTHER JACK:

*English don and brother of C.S. Lewis, 1895–1973*

Variety may be the spice of life, but it is monotony that brings home the groceries.

---

# MALCOLM FORBES TO HIS SON, STEVE:

*American publisher and businessman, 1919–1990*

If you have a job without aggravations, you don't have a job.

---

# ALBERT EINSTEIN TO THE PHYSICIST GEORGE TRUETT:

*German-born American theoretical physicist, 1879–1955*

The idle man does not know what it is to enjoy rest.

# KNG SOLOMON TO HIS SON:

*King of Israel, Tenth century B.C.*

My son, ill-gotten gains do not profit, but righteousness delivers from death. The Lord will not allow the righteous to hunger, but He will thrust aside the craving of the wicked. Poor is he who works with a negligent hand, but the hand of the diligent makes rich. The soul of the sluggard craves and gets nothing, but the soul of the diligent is made fat. Wealth obtained by fraud dwindles, but the one who gathers by labor increases it. A man can do nothing better than find satisfaction in his work.

---

# MARTIN LUTHER TO PHILIP MELANCHTHON:

*German theologian and leader of the Reformation, 1483–1546*

The world does not consider labor a blessing, therefore, it flees and hates it but the pious who fear the Lord, labor with a ready and cheerful heart; for they know God's command and will, they acknowledge His calling.

# COTTON MATHER TO HIS SON, SAMUEL:

*⊶ American Colonial author and theologian, 1663–1728 ⊷*

A Christian should follow his occupation with contentment. Is your business here clogged with any difficulties and inconveniences? Contentment under those difficulties is no little part of your homage to that King who hath placed you where you are by His call.

---

# WILLIAM TYNDALE TO HIS PATRON LORD ARGYLE:

*⊶ English Bible translator and martyr, 1494–1536 ⊷*

If we look externally there is a difference betwixt the washing of dishes and preaching of the Word of God; but as touching to please God, in relation to His call, none at all.

---

# HENRY FORD TO THOMAS EDISON:

*⊶ American automobile manufacturer, 1863–1947 ⊷*

Genius is seldom recognized for what it is: a great capacity for hard work.

# Hugh Latimer to a young catechumen in his church:
*⊰ English pastor, Reformer, and martyr, 1485–1555 ⊱*

Our Saviour, Christ Jesus, was a carpenter and got His living with great labor. Therefore, let no man disdain to follow Him in a common calling and occupation.

---

# Noel Coward to a young actress:
*⊰ British actor, playwright, and composer, 1899–1973 ⊱*

Work is much more fun than fun.

---

# Andy Tant to his fellow classmates:
*⊰ American student, 1980–1996 ⊱*

If your ship doesn't come in, swim out to it.

# N otes

FRONTMATTER
*Page 9:* Hillaire Belloc, A Belloc Omnibus, (London: Harrell and Jones, 1955), p. 132; James Rawls, The Southern Agrarians, (Memphis: Forrester and Blanchard, 1971), p. 55; *page 11:* Martin Bealles, *Letters of the Heart*, (London: Cassell, 1928), p. 122; *page 13: Ibid.*, p. 209.

ANGER
*Page 18:* Thomas Helton, *The Art of Correspondence*, (London: Willis and Gonnic, 1937), p. 209; Charles Villard, *American Letters*, (Boston: Gavin Fulcher, 1956), p. 175; George Talbot-Rees, *Great Letters from Great Writers*, (New York: Felquart Brothers, 1977), p. 2; *page 19:* Helton, p. 37; *page 20: Ibid.*, p. 99; Talbot-Rees, p. 302.

CHARACTER
*Page 22:* Robert Payne, *The Image of Chekov, Forty Stories of Anton Chekov in the Order in Which They Were Written*, (New York: Knopf, 1976), p. 12; M. Lincoln Schuster, ed., *A Treasury of the World's Great Letters*, (New York: Simon and Schuster, 1940), p. 371; *pages 23-24:* Thomas Carlyle, *Oliver Cromwell's Letters & Speeches with Elucidations*, (London: J.M. Dent, 1897), p. 77; *page 25:* Villard, p. 48; *pages 25-26:* Frank and Anita Kermode, eds., *The Oxford Book of Letters*, (London: Oxford University Press, 1996), p. 232; *pages 27-29: ibid.*, p. 58; *page 30:* Villard, p. 40; Helton, p. 77.

CHILDREN
*Pages 32-40:* Rebecca Lamar Harmon, *Susanna, Mother of the Wesleys*, (Nashville, Tennessee: Abingdon Press, 1968), p. 246; *page 40:* Villard, p. 191.

COURAGE
*Page 42:* Helton, p. 117; Theodore Roosevelt, *The Complete Works, vol. XIX,* (New York: Charles Scribner's Sons, 1926), p. 331; *page 43:* Villard, p. 77; Helton, p. 245; *page 44: Ibid.,* p. 231; *pages 45-46:* George Grant, *Immaculate Deception,* (Chicago, Illinois: Northfield, 1996), p. 66.

DEATH
*Page 48: The Life Advocate,* June 1991; Helton, p. 184; *pages 49-52: Ibid.,* p. 148; *page 52: Ibid.,* p. 222; *page 53,* Villard, p. 232; Helton, p. 330; *pages 54-58:* Schuster, p. 314.

EDUCATION
*Page 60:* Florence MacCunn, *Sir Walter Scott's Friends,* (New York: John Lane, 1910), p. 244; Villard, p. 341; *Ibid.,* p. xii; *page 61:* Helton, p. 84; Talbot-Rees, p. 55; *page 62: Ibid.,* p. 56; *Ibid.,* p. 61; *page 63:* Helton, p. 86; *page 64:* 1 Corinthians 10:11; Talbot-Rees, p. 56; Villard, p. 77.

FAITH
*Pages 66-69:* Robert Speaight, ed., *Letters from Hilaire Belloc,* (New York: MacMillan, 1958), p. 154; *page 70:* George Lewis Prentiss, *More Love to Thee: The Life and Letters of Elizabeth Prentiss,* (Amityville, New York, Calvary Press, 1994), p. 289; *page 71:* Talbot-Rees, P. 227; 2 Timothy 4:7.

FOOD
*Page 73:* Martha Jones-Holbert, *Talking about Taste,* (New York: Bear and Bristle, 1990), p. 33; *Ibid.; pages 74-78:* Julia M. Pitkin, Karen Grant, and George Grant, *Bless This Food,* (Nashville, Tennessee: Cumberland House, 1996), p. 11; *page 79:* Villard, p. 105.

FORGIVENESS
*Page 81:* Talbot-Rees, p. 326; LeRoy Untermeyer, *A Song of Justice,* (Los Angeles, California: Mere and Kallis, 1988), p. 49; *pages 82-83:* Corrie Ten

Boom, *Prison Letters*, (Old Tappan, New Jersey: Revell, 1975), p. 43; *page 83:* Villard, p. 78.

FREEDOM
*Pages 85-87:* James Boswell, *Life of Johnson*, (New York: Thomas Y. Crowell, 1914), p. 432; *page 87:* Villard, p. 248; *pages 88-104:* George Grant, ed., *The Patriot's Handbook*, (Nashville, Tennessee: Cumberland House, 1996), pp. 422-429; *pages 105-107:* George Grant, *KMSC Collection*, (Franklin, Tennessee: KMSC, 1997), p. 9.

GARDENS
*Pages 109-111:* Anne Scott-James and Clare Hastings, *Gardening Letters to My Daughter*, (New York: St. Martin's Press, 1990), p. 64; *pages 112-114;* Ibid., p. 88; *pages 115-117:* George Grant, *Micah Mandate*, (Chicago: Moody, 1995). p. 47.

GRIEF
*Pages 119-120:* Talbot-Rees, p. 159; *pages 120-121:* Asa Cummings, *A Memoir of the Rev. Edward Payson*, (New York: American Tract Society, 1830), p. 77; *page 122:* W. Robertson Nicoll, *Ian MacLaren, Life of the Rev. John Watson*, (London: Hodder and Stoughton, 1908), p. 156.

JUSTICE
*Pages 124-126:* Villard, p. 194; *pages 127-128:* Armand deFellier, *A Presidential Omnibus*, (Cincinnati, Ohio: Graber and Sons, 1967), p. 70; *page 128:* Villard, p. 182; Micah 6:8.

LEADERSHIP
*Pages 130-132:* Frank and Anita Kermode, eds., *The Oxford Book of Letters*, (London: Oxford University Press, 1996), p. 232; *page 132:* Villard, p. 99; *page 133:* Thomas Carlyle, *Oliver Cromwell's Letters & Speeches with Elucidations*, (London: J.M. Dent, 1897), p. 291.

LIFE
*Page 135:* Helton, 209; *Ibid,* p. 49; Talbot-Rees, p. 56; *pages 136-140:* Robert Burns, *The Poetical Works of Robert Burns,* (London: Frederick Warne, 1892), p. 134; *page 140:* Romans 12: 9-12; *page 141:* Villard, p. 247; *Ibid.,* p. 175; Helton. p. 44.

LOVE
*Page 143:* Talbot-Rees, p. 167; Burns, p. 144; Helton, p. 204; *page 144: Ibid.,* p. 166; *Ibid.,* p. 168; *pages 145-146: Ibid.,* p. 134; *pages 147-148: Ibid.,* p. 322; *pages 149-150:* Proberbs 5: 1-23; *pages 150-151:* 1 Corinthians 13: 1-13; *pages 152-153:* Talbot-Rees, p. 281.

MARRIAGE
*Page 157:* Elizabeth Gaskell, *The Life of Charlotte Brontë,* (London: Penguin Books, 1985), p. 184; *page 158:* Helton, p. 55; George Gavin Holt, *Love and Life: Letters,* (New York: Ballaustride, 1988), p. 166; *pages 159-162:* Villard, p. 38.

MONEY
*Pages 164-166:* Helton, p. 197; *page 166:* Villard, p. 44; *Ibid.,* p. 100; *page 167: Ibid.,* p. 101; *Ibid.; Ibid.,* p. 102; *page 168:* Talbot-Rees, p. 277; *page 169:* Proverbs 6:1-11; *pages 170-171:* Asa Cummings, *A Memoir of the Rev. Edward Payson,* (New York: American Tract Society, 1830), p. 88; *page 171:* Talbot-Rees, p. ix.

READING
*Page 173:* Lyman Abbott, *The Guide to Reading,* (Garden City, New York: Nelson Doubleday, 1924), p. 36; *Ibid.,* p. 45; *page 174: Ibid,* p. 45; *Ibid.,* p. 16; *page 175:* Theodore Roosevelt, *The Complete Works, vol. XIX,* (New York: Charles Scribner's Sons, 1926), p. 322; *pages 176-184:* Thomas Jefferson, *A Virginia Gentleman's Library,* (Williamsburg, Virginia: Colonial Williamsburg, 1990), pp. 9-15; *pages 185-186:* Abbott, pp. xxi-xxv; *page 187:*

Abbott, p. 3; *Ibid.*, p. 56; Talbot-Rees, p. 88; *page 188:* Abbott, p. 77; *Ibid.*, p. 81.

RELATIVES
*Page 190:* Helton, p. 20; *pages 191-192:* Schuster, p. 287.

SPORT
*Page 194:* I Timothy 4:8; *pages 194-197:* Roosevelt, p. 341; *page 197:* Villard, p. 343

TACT
*Page 199: New York Times,* July 17, 1988; Villard, p. 166; *Ibid.*, p. 56; *page 200:* Helton, p. 69; *page 201:* Villard, p. iv; W. Robertson Nicoll, *Ian MacLaren, Life of the Rev. John Watson,* (London: Hodder and Stoughton, 1908), p. 278; *page 202:* Helton, p. 71; *Ibid.*

TEMPTATION
*Pages 205-206:* Villard, p. 177; *page 206:* Talbot-Rees, p. 28; *Ibid.*, p. 32; *page 207:* Villard, p. 284; *Ibid.*, p. 62; Nicoll, p. 122.

TRIALS
*Page 209:* Villard, p. 166; Talbot-Rees, p. 76; *Ibid.*, p. 244; *pages 210-213:* *Ibid.*, pp. 241-243; *page 214:* Schuster, p. 57; Nicoll, p. 122.

WORK
*Page 216:* Talbot-Rees, p. 254; *Ibid.*, p. 294; *Ibid.*, p. 187; *page 217:* Proverbs 10: 2-5; Kevin Latimer, *The Puritan Doctrine of Work,* (London: Christian Banner, 1971), p. 47; *page 218: Ibid.*, p. 49; *Ibid.*, p. 48; Talbot-Rees, p. 185; *page 219:* Latimer, p. 45; Talbot-Rees, p. 180; Franklin Classical School *Mercury,* Spring 1997.